W9-ABG-185

Key Resources
on Student Services

Albert B. Hood
Cathann Arceneaux

Z
5814
.P8
H75
1990

Key Resources
on Student Services

A Guide
to the Field
and Its Literature

Jossey-Bass Publishers

San Francisco • Oxford • 1990

KVCC KALAMAZOO VALLEY
COMMUNITY COLLEGE
LIBRARY

KEY RESOURCES ON STUDENT SERVICES
A Guide to the field and Its Literature
  by Albert B. Hood and Cathann Arceneaux

Copyright © 1990 by: Jossey-Bass Inc., Publishers
                    350 Sansome Street
                    San Francisco, California 94104
                        &
                    Jossey-Bass Limited
                    Headington Hill Hall
                    Oxford OX3 0BW

Copyright under International, Pan American, and
Universal Copyright Conventions. All rights
reserved. No part of this book may be reproduced
in any form—except for brief quotation (not to
exceed 1,000 words) in a review or professional
work—without permission in writing from the publishers.

Library of Congress Cataloging-in-Publication Data

Hood, Albert B. (Albert Bullard), date.
    Key resources on student services: a guide to the field and its
literature / Albert B. Hood, Cathann Arceneaux.
       p. cm. — (The Jossey-Bass higher education series)
    ISBN 1-55542-230-6
    1. Personnel service in higher education—United States—
Bibliography.   2. College student development programs—United
States—Bibliography.   I. Arceneaux, Cathann.   II. Title.
III. Series.
Z5814.P8H75 1990
[LB2343]
016.3781'94'0973—dc20
                                                        89-48168
                                                       CIP

Manufactured in the United States of America

The paper in this book meets the guidelines for
permanence and durability of the Committee on
Production Guidelines for Book Longevity of
the Council on Library Resources.

JACKET DESIGN BY WILLI BAUM

FIRST EDITION

Code 9029

The Jossey-Bass
Higher Education Series

Contents

Preface

The total content of professional, scientific, and academic literature may be likened to an enormous, ever expanding universe. Within this universe are many general subject areas, or galaxies, within which are more specialized solar systems — each with a number of particular specialties, or planets. Many of these galaxies and solar systems encompass areas of knowledge widely separated from others, although some of them are close enough to exert considerable influence on each other. One of these galaxies is higher education, and within that galaxy lies the student services solar system. Fields such as psychology, sociology, counseling, and administration, although existing in totally different galaxies, have overlapping orbits with the student affairs solar system. The counseling psychology solar system within the psychology galaxy lies in an orbit that overlaps considerably with the student affairs solar system. Within the student affairs solar system there are a large number of planets which include, for example, financial aid, career services and placement, and academic advising. This volume presents an overview of the principal sources of literature in the student services solar system, including that of each of its planets.

Continuously expanding knowledge bases and increased specialization of activities have resulted in the subdivision of many professions into substantive specialties, and the student services profession is no exception. As the student services field becomes more specialized, the particular specialties or planets will become larger in size and, in a constantly expanding uni-

verse, continue to draw away from one another. A large body
of literature has developed in certain specialties, such as financial aid, admissions, or career services. Smaller amounts of
specialized literature, some of which will undoubtedly grow
substantially during the next decades, are found in such specialties as student activities and new student orientation.

Purpose of the Book

The different services — or planets — in the student affairs
field and their accompanying literature will continue to become
more specialized as communication decreases among them. A
primary purpose of this volume is to provide assistance to professionals who wish to undertake interplanetary space travel
within the ever expanding student affairs field. The literature,
even as it has become more specialized, will continue to grow
rapidly. This expansion can be explained in part because student services professionals are found on college and university
campuses where scholarship and research are valued. In addition, the major research universities, through promotion policies
that require research and publication, have acted (whether de-
liberately or not) to ensure the production and dissemination
of knowledge (whether significant and relevant or not) within
the various academic and professional fields, which include student services. But even without this pressure to publish, the
literature in the field would still continue to grow rapidly because
for any profession to remain vital, new knowledge must be produced and shared. As a result of the discovering and sharing
of new information, professional services improve, providing
ultimate benefits to constituents, related institutions, and society.
The student services field is made up primarily of practitioners, and thus most of the significant resources in student
services are aimed at the practitioner as a knowledge consumer.
However, practitioners are very busy professionals with little
time for research and writing, and they typically favor working
with people over the more solitary activities of research and
writing. Thus a substantial portion of the literature in the student services field is produced either by university professors

(or their students) or by individuals commissioned by professional associations. Since scholarship and publication are the primary means of career advancement for university professors, a substantial proportion of journal articles and books are produced by faculty who prepare student affairs professionals.

The literature in student services differs from that in the typical scientific or academic field. As an applied profession, student services makes use of knowledge developed by the basic areas of the social sciences. In the same way that those in an applied field such as medicine make use of knowledge developed in a wide variety of basic sciences — pathology, biochemistry, genetics, and the life sciences — and apply this knowledge to the treatment of their patients, the student services practitioner takes the knowledge generated in many disciplines — typically in such social sciences as psychology and sociology — and applies it to enhancing the education and development of college students. Thus the major function of the professional field's literature is to disseminate knowledge from basic disciplines that is relevant to student services and to describe theories and techniques that can be used to accomplish the missions of the various student services agencies on the campus.

An attempt to review the literature of a particular profession is not an easy task since the profession is likely to have a long history and include a number of broad areas. Many arbitrary decisions must be made regarding which resources are current, which are out of date, which are central to the task at hand, and which are peripheral.

The intent of this book is to briefly describe only the significant recent sources of literature in the student services field. The list of possible literature citations consists of thousands of journal articles, thousands of summaries of conference and convention presentations, and many essays and columns from association newsletters, so no attempt has been made to provide a comprehensive review of these types of resources. While a small amount of literature in this field began to be produced early in this century, most has been produced during the past twenty-five or thirty years. However, it is within the last decade that the greatest increase has occurred, for as the professionalization of the various specialties within the student services field has substantially increased, the various types of sources of literature have proliferated as well. Consequently, the resources we present consist primarily of the larger, more significant sources and literature that has been produced during recent years. A few important sources produced prior to 1980 have been referenced, but, in general, books and monographs published since 1980 are included. Few journal articles are included, and sources such as speeches, dissertations, and institutional reports are not included, nor are those reports and presentations available only through the ERIC system. Instead, we attempted to include as many of the significant books and extensive monographs as possible. The various journals are cited and information is provided about them, but specific articles appearing in them have typically not been noted.

Organization of the Book

Key Resources on Student Services is organized according to the specialty areas within the student services field. Within each specialty area the literature sources have been further divided by subject. The introduction to each of the chapters presents a brief overview of the literature in that specialty and discusses the issues and trends within that specialty, as revealed by the literature. The list of sources is selective—it includes only significant resources. Those works considered to be of indispensable value and important to anyone wishing to gain knowledge in that specialty are marked by stars (★).

This book is intended to be useful for different purposes and for different audiences. Those who wish to obtain a general impression of the student services field can do so by browsing through the book, paying particular attention to the subsections within each chapter. Each of the chapter introductions provides information about both the field as a whole and the specialty areas within it. Readers who need information about a specialty will find the particular chapter a most useful reference to learn where to obtain resources that deal with their subject of interest. Readers with a more general interest in material related to a

particular chapter should make use of the starred references—
these are the significant resources in that chapter. Graduate
students will be able to locate references useful to them in the
different specialties, and new professionals who need to become
more knowledgeable about the area in which they are employed
will find the references particularly valuable.

The major criteria for referencing works in this book were
(1) significance to professionals in the field and (2) recency of
publication date—since 1980. Works written for students or for
the lay public are not included, and only a few particularly important resources published prior to 1980 are referenced. An-
notations are relatively short in length and are designed to
present only a brief overview of the content of the work—they
are not meant to constitute a critical review. In order to be
referenced in this volume, works had to be considered useful
to professionals. Resources that are important to professionals
in several areas are cross-referenced between chapters.

The first four chapters contain references useful for professionals in all the different specialties within student services
while the next eight chapters are related to a particular specialty.
These eight chapters are arranged in the order in which the
undergraduate student might have contact with them, beginning with recruitment and admissions and ending with career
services and placement.

Chapter One presents a brief history of the field, along
with an overview of the literature within it. Chapter Two contains references pertaining to the organization and structure of
the profession. Chapter Three, a somewhat lengthy chapter, contains resources that present various student development theories
and their applications, along with resources that describe college students and their characteristics. References that deal with
the administration of student services and aspects of general administration in higher education are listed in Chapter Four.
Chapter Five lists resources in the general field of enrollment
management, breaking them down into the areas with which
enrollment management is concerned—recruitment, admissions,
orientation, and retention. Resources in the areas of student
financial aid, residence life, academic advising and learning

assistance services, and international student services are contained in Chapters Six through Nine. There is a vast literature in the field of counseling, and so it was necessary to list only those works that deal specifically with college counseling centers in Chapter Ten. Resources related to student activities and college unions are included in Chapter Eleven. Chapter Twelve contains not only references that deal with placement but also those that are concerned with career development and career services. Chapter Thirteen examines emerging issues and trends in the field.

Acknowledgments

A special word of thanks to Reta Litton and Ginny Travis for their word processing of many drafts as the manuscript evolved from a miscellaneous collection of references into organized chapters.

We also want to express our deep appreciation to our families, particularly Jean Hood and Milton and Charlotte Winborn, for their understanding of our reduced attention to social and home maintenance schedules during the period that this manuscript was being prepared.

Iowa City, Iowa   Albert B. Hood
January 1990   Cathann Arceneaux

The Authors

Albert B. Hood is professor of education and director of the Student Development Program in Postsecondary Education at the University of Iowa. He received his B.A. degree (1951) from the University of New Hampshire in psychology and his Ed.D. degree (1957) from Cornell University in counseling and student personnel administration.

He has been a residence hall director at both the University of New Hampshire and Cornell University, and at Princeton University he was the assistant director of the Student Counseling Service and a member of the psychology department. Prior to his current assignment, he was a counseling psychologist in the Student Counseling Bureau and a member of the department of educational psychology at the University of Minnesota. He has held a research fellowship in Kyoto, Japan, and has been a visiting faculty member at the University of Utah and San Francisco State University.

Author of more than ninety books, monographs, and professional articles, Hood received the Contribution to Knowledge Award of the American College Personnel Association (ACPA) in 1985. He was the editor of the ACPA's *Journal of College Student Personnel* from 1970 to 1976 and also served the ACPA as a member of the executive council and as the treasurer. He is a fellow in the American Psychological Association's Division 17 (Counseling). Hood's scholarly work deals primarily with research on the psychological, educational, and vocational development of college students, and most of the over fifty Ph.D. dissertations he has directed have dealt with this topic.

Cathann Arceneaux is completing a residency in clinical pastoral education at the University of Iowa Hospitals and Clinics, and she is a candidate in the Ph.D. program in the Student Development Program in Postsecondary Education at the University of Iowa.

She received her B.S. degree (1983) from Iowa State University in social work and her M.S. degree (1986) from the University of Iowa in education. While completing her graduate study, she has been a residence hall director at Iowa State University and the Learning Center Coordinator for Women's Athletics at the University of Iowa. In addition, from 1987 to 1989, she was a part-time faculty member at Kirkwood Community College in Iowa City. She has also been a research fellow through Iowa Testing Programs (1986–1989), a teaching assistant in the Connie Belin National Center for Gifted Education, and most recently the acting director for the Counseling Lab for Talent Development (1988–1989).

She is currently researching the emotional development of underachieving gifted students and developing interventions geared toward assisting students to make meaningful vocational decisions.

Key Resources
on Student Services

Emergence of
Student Services
Practice and Literature

Three developments in American higher education contributed to the emergence of the student personnel field (Fenske in Delworth and Hanson, 1989, no. 13). First, there was a shift from a religious to a more secular orientation of institutions. Originally charged with the responsibility of developing both a student's intellect and character, the religiously oriented institutions incorporated student services into their structure. As this orientation waned, institutions began hiring new staff members whose sole responsibility was to support and serve students outside the classroom.

Concurrently, a second development was the expansion in size and complexity of the institutions themselves. Thirdly, as a result of these changes, the faculties shifted their focus from student development to academic concerns. These developments bolstered the trend toward the hiring of professionals designated to serve students' needs. In the brief history that follows, these three developments will be considered as a way of organizing the historical changes.

A Brief History

The British college served as the model for European settlers when they first established institutions of higher education

1

in America. Harvard College was fashioned after Emmanuel College in Cambridge University; it was similarly built not in Boston itself but in a rural area across the river. These early colleges fostered a holistic educational philosophy that emphasized morality and character as well as the intellect, and therefore by their very nature were student service oriented. As a result of the rural location of many colleges, there was a need for institutions to provide lodging, board, and leisure activities. Many of the colleges were affiliated with churches with usually the president, and some of the faculty, being members of the clergy.

In contrast, the European universities were (and still are) located in major cities and had typically older students, who found their own lodgings and extracurricular activities throughout the city. During the latter half of the nineteenth century, an increasing number of Americans returned from advanced study in Germany to become members of American faculties. The influence of the German universities, which fostered academic and personal independence and resolutely left students to their own devices outside the classroom setting, introduced many conflicting ideas about the educational objectives within the residential college. Furthermore, graduate schools staffed by Ph.D.'s, many of whom had trained in scientific fields in German universities, were added to some American colleges. This focus on science, engineering, and the new social sciences involved a heavy emphasis upon research, and many colleges and universities became more impersonal and secular, emphasizing intellectual pursuits and professional specialization rather than genteel character building. While most small liberal arts colleges did not change over and become universities with centers of graduate, research, and professional education, they were influenced by the changes because faculties were almost always selected from universities. With these changes, student counseling, advising, and support, once the responsibility of faculty, ceased to be viewed as a faculty priority.

In addition, two catalysts that contributed to the shift from a more religious to secular orientation came with the Dartmouth College case and the Yale Report. In 1816 the Dartmouth College case set a precedent for distinguishing between private, often religious institutions and the public institutions run by the state. The import of this case was that the state could not interfere with the college charter, clearly delineating the separation of church and state. With this separation, more energy was invested in clearly delineating secular from religious, and the original philosophy of holistic education was replaced by a sense of academic responsibility. The Yale Report, published in 1828, was an assertion of the humanist tradition. Its major points included a defense of the classics, the necessity for a liberal arts education for all, and a plea for quality in education. This report, with its focus on the curriculum, helped liberate the American college from excessive religious orientation and move toward a focus on liberal arts.

In 1862 the first Morrill Land-Grant Act provided that eligible states would receive public land or negotiable scrip for each member of the state's congressional delegation. Proceeds were to provide a permanent endowment for at least one college that would teach subjects related to the agricultural or mechanical arts. The second Morrill Land-Grant Act of 1890 provided annual financial appropriations and required that the institutions must be accessible to all people, regardless of race. These increases created a need for more student services professionals to meet the needs of the new constituency of students attending higher education institutions.

Higher education's concern with the whole student increased again after the turn of the century. Knowledge gained from psychology regarding individual differences, faculty members' increasing preoccupation with their subject matter fields, and new educational functions all resulted in the appointment of persons to perform such duties as educational and vocational counseling and advising, placement, student health, and extracurricular activities. Furthermore, as institutions became larger, certain student services such as registration and admissions could no longer be carried out by part-time faculty members and, consequently, full-time personnel were appointed. As these professional specialties emerged, they founded professional associations. Early associations were for registrars, the American Association of Collegiate Registrars and Admissions Officers (AACRAO);

for counselors, the American Personnel and Guidance Association (APGA), which later became the American Association for Counseling and Development (AACD); and for placement officers, the College Placement Council (CPC). Deans of women and deans of men organized the National Association for Women Deans, Administrators, and Counselors (NAWDAC) and the National Association of Deans and Administrators of Men (NADAM), which later became the National Association of Student Personnel Administrators (NASPA). When the first major statement of *The Student Personnel Point of View* (no. 14) was written in 1937, its authors listed twenty-three different functions or services important to meet the needs of individual students.

In 1946 the Truman Commission reviewed the condition of education after World War II and called for institutions with more geographic and pedagogical accessibility. This led to emergence of community colleges and urged the provision of financial aid so that racial, ethnic, and financial barriers could be removed.

The end of World War II brought about a great expansion in the numbers of students in higher education institutions, primarily due to the GI Bill. This bill, the most direct expression of widening opportunity for higher education, entitled all veterans to financial support for direct college costs and subsistence upon their enrollment in an accredited college or university. Along with this widening opportunity for students came the need for increasing specialization to perform the various student personnel functions in admissions, counseling and testing, residence services, and student unions. Eventually, professional associations emerged in some of these different services: for financial aid, the National Association of Student Financial Aid Administrators (NASFAA); for foreign student advising, the National Association for Foreign Student Affairs (NAFSA); for union management, the Association of College Unions-International (ACU-I); and for housing, the Association of College and University Housing Officers (ACUHO). The 1949 statement of *The Student Personnel Point of View* (no. 14) revised the previous statement regarding the philosophical basis for student personnel work and outlined the elements for a comprehensive institutional program. During the next decade, the specialty areas in student services continued to become established as professionals attempted to respond to the 1949 statement.

In the 1960s, with the increasing number of students as a result of the baby boom, higher education experienced a tremendous expansion. Similarly, the student services profession expanded and moved from informal centers staffed perhaps with only one person to formal centers with administrative levels and staff.

Recent Influences

Institutions of higher education experienced considerable social upheaval in the 1960s, due in part to the large number of students. Student services professionals often found themselves involved with student activism, as the institutional liaison. Furthermore, changing attitudes began to redirect the role of student services, including the demise of *in loco parentis,* the view of students as immature and in need of guidance and supervision from the institution taking responsibility for them. Beginning in 1968, the Tomorrow's Higher Education Project, a planned response to higher education changes, called for examining the future of college student services. It resulted in the Brown monograph (no. 17) published in 1972, outlining nine alternative roles for student personnel workers. This monograph, *Student Development in Tomorrow's Higher Education: A Return to the Academy,* emphasized the need to recognize that student development is a total campus effort and not the exclusive province of those in the profession. It recommended that the profession should establish direct ties with the academic faculty and become expert in such areas as learning theory, development, and campus ecology. It also stressed the need for new research.

In 1975 the Council of Student Personnel Associations (COSPA), representing all the different associations, prepared a statement delineating five important tenets of the profession. Although COSPA disbanded soon after, the statement represents the one time that all the associations of the myriad specialty areas banded together. The five tenets agreed upon include maintaining a developmental perspective, fostering student self-direction as a goal, viewing students as collaborators in the learning process, understanding the variety of theoretical approaches, and maintaining a proactive position regarding students' needs.

Terminology and Identity

In order to put the relevant literature in this field in perspective, one must first understand a central issue unique to this profession, an issue involving the very identity of the profession. The literature reflects the confusion this field has often experienced in attempting to clarify its major roles and responsibilities and in separating itself from the general field of higher education. Clearly, this can be seen in the lack of consensus on the name of this field.

Originally comprised primarily of deans, most professionals designated their field as *student affairs*. This term reflected their concern with what students were doing outside the classroom and for students' general well-being. With the development and use of psychological testing originating in France, the term *student personnel* became more popular and was further bolstered by the publication of the cornerstone 1937 American Council on Education statement, *The Student Personnel Point of View* (no. 14), which provided a comprehensive statement of student services beliefs and was accepted as a guide for professional development. As a partial result of criticism that the term *personnel* was reminiscent of *office personnel,* many in the field adopted the term *student services* to emphasize the variety of roles and the service aspect of the profession. With the more recent major push in the field toward adopting a holistic attitude emphasizing the total development of the student in contrast to other higher education areas that focus either on intellectual development or the economics of higher education, the term *student development* became more popular.

This shift in terms to designate the profession illustrates

the shift in the focus of the field, which has moved from the original control function of discipline to a diversity of service functions and finally to a more developmental perspective. Although a developmental theory and general philosophy have now become the conceptual guideline for the field, throughout the literature these four terms — *student affairs, student personnel, student services,* and *student development* — continue to be used interchangeably and, correspondingly, they are used interchangeably in this bibliography.

The identity confusion in the student services profession can also be seen in the gradual emergence of the field. The first student services worker could be identified as the Yale tutor who subsisted on the fines he collected from disobedient students. Deans of students followed and as women began attending, deans of women. The primary period of emergence for the profession was from the Civil War to World War I. However, the era of greatest growth occurred in the years after World War I and ended with the Depression of the 1930s. A period of inertia followed due to cutbacks and a change in the academic philosophy in the 1930s. Since then, the profession has regained its pattern of growth in size, but different specialties are often widely separated on the campus. With each particular service focusing on different aspects of the total student, the student services professional often feels a strong sense of isolation from other student services professionals. In addition, an enduring sense that student services is incidental to the "real" work of the institution has continued to plague many professionals, still searching for ways to become more integrated with the academic enterprise.

The Evolution of Professional Literature

The early literature in the field tended to be quite meager and was typically made up of stories, anecdotes, and reminiscences and advice from deans; recommendations regarding record keeping to promote common and consistent practices regarding grades, semester hours, and graduation requirements; admissions requirements and admissions testing; and eventually some literature regarding the counseling of students. This early literature was usually in the form of conference proceedings and books such as *Through a Dean's Open Door* (Hawkes and Hawkes, 1945). The quantity of literature in the field began to grow, slowly in the late 1940s, but it was only in the 1950s that rapid expansion began in earnest. Several books were published, various journals in the field were initiated by the various growing professional associations, and a number of other organizations were founded to deal with specific concerns of higher education.

The American Council of Education, the source of the two statements of *The Student Personnel Point of View,* included monographs dealing with aspects of student affairs among their publications. Considerable research dealing with the matriculation in college of able students on a national level were produced in the 1950s by the College Entrance Examination Board (CEEB) along with the Educational Testing Service, which conducted and published various studies dealing with admissions and financial aids. Project Talent, which developed out of the reaction to Sputnik in the early 1960s, was designed to measure talent in a test sample of students and looked at abilities and college matriculation. Beginning in the early 1960s additional organizations, such as the American College Testing Program, the Center for the Study of Higher Education in California, the Western Interstate Commission for Higher Education (WICHE), to name only a few, also began to make substantial contributions to the literature in the student services field. Furthermore, periodic reports relating to the field were produced by the Carnegie Commission.

As institutions of higher education became larger, additional professionals were needed in the student services field to provide individual assistance within the large institutions. As university faculties became increasingly concerned with scholarship, research, and publication, faculty members had less time to devote to students — particularly undergraduate students — so additional staff members were needed to assume these supporting responsibilities. Within the national student services associations, interest groups within the various specialties began to form, soon separating from the parent associations and then

beginning to publish their own books, monographs, and journals, and to provide a literature base within each of the student
services specialties. In 1922 the *Vocational Guidance Journal* was
started; in 1952 it evolved into the *Personnel and Guidance Journal*
and eventually in 1984 into the *Journal of Counseling and Development* (no. 503). In 1937 the National Association for Women
Deans, Administrators, and Counselors (NAWDAC) began
publishing the *Journal of the National Association for Women Deans,
Administrators, and Counselors* (no. 2). In 1945 the *Personnel-O-Gram*
was established, changing in 1959 to the *Journal of College Student Personnel* and most recently in 1989 to the *Journal of College
Student Development* (no. 1). Other specialized journals were
established in the early 1970s, including the *Journal of College
and University Student Housing* (no. 501). Certain of these specialized fields, such as financial aids and placement, have established
strong national organizations that actively communicate with
their members and provide a variety of different types of professional literature within their respective field. Other specialized
fields, such as student activities and orientation, have been slower
to organize and have yet to establish national associations that
contribute substantial amounts of literature. The literature that
exists in such fields as these comes from other sources and from
other professional associations.

   During the late 1960s and early 1970s there was a great
outpouring of literature dealing with college students. Psychologists, sociologists, political scientists, journalists, and philos-
ophers all studied and wrote about the causes and results of
student unrest and about the characteristics and activities of the
student activist. Although some of this writing is found in the
student affairs literature, the majority of it was written by those
from other disciplines and appeared in such books as *The New
Student Left: An Anthology* (Cohen and Hale, 1966) and *The Berkeley
Student Revolt: Facts and Interpretations* (Lipset and Wolin, 1965).

   Periodically within the field of student services there has
been produced a book that attempted to summarize what was
known at that particular time about the student services field.
Two of the earliest books that did not attempt to cover the broad
field but that were still influential were Williamson's *How to*

Counsel Students in 1939 and Williamson and Foley's *Counseling and Discipline* in 1949. An early book that discussed the entire field of student services was Wrenn's *Student Personnel Work in College*, which appeared in 1951. The next similar work, published in 1961, was Kate Mueller's *Student Personnel Work in Higher Education. College Student Personnel* (Fitzgerald, Johnson and Norris), published in 1970, also dealt with the entire field of student services, as did the book edited by Packwood (no. 27) in 1977, which summarized the research literature available in sixteen aspects or specialties within the field. The most recent generalist volume is that of Delworth and Hanson (no. 23), first published in 1980 and now in its 1989 second edition.

Recommendations for Future Literature

Besides those major books, the literature contains many small studies, brief descriptions of programs, survey results, and professional issues within specialties but tends not to include thoughtful summaries of research, critical reviews of research in the field, or theoretical or conceptual formulations. These larger, more comprehensive contributions to the literature are what appear to be needed in the student services field rather than more smaller studies produced by professors and graduate students. More writing is also needed by thoughtful practitioners who conceptualize, analyze, and critically review the roles, activities, and theories as they carry out their duties. Also needed are empirical practitioners who study and evaluate the activities they attempt to accomplish on their campuses.

As mentioned earlier, the role of professional associations in the production of literature has taken on increased importance, particularly during the last decade. The number of specialties within the student services field that have organized into professional organizations with a sizable membership and therefore adequate finances to produce literature useful to practitioners within that specialty has grown in great, if not alarming, proportions. On the one hand, this has resulted in the dissemination of large amounts of knowledge to specialized practitioners; however, it has also resulted in an increased specialization through the literature of student services professionals already in isolation from one another in regard to communication on the campus.

As this specialization continues to evolve, the need for books and monographs that present concepts, theories, and research that can influence the entire field will grow. The mission of the generalist journals in student affairs should also change. The role of publishing essays and research studies dealing with specialized areas is being taken over by the journals produced by the specialized professional associations. The editors of the generalist journals should therefore attempt to provide literature that will provide communication across the specialties and include those theoretical and research articles significant for those throughout the profession.

Periodical Literature

In the student services field there are three generalist publications that present conceptual formulations, research, and activities from a number of the various specialties. These are the following:

1   *Journal of College Student Development* (formerly *Journal of College Student Personnel*). Published six times a year by the American College Personnel Association, 5999 Stevenson Avenue, Alexandria, Va. 22304.

Subscription to this journal is included with American College Personnel Association membership. It publishes essays and research reports related to professional interests and responsibilities of college student personnel/development professionals.

2   *Initiatives* formerly *Journal of the National Association for Women Deans, Administrators, and Counselors).* Published quarterly by the National Association for Women Deans, Administrators, and Counselors, 1325 Eighteenth Street NW, Suite 210, Washington, D.C. 20036.

Articles in this journal include a wide range of studies and issues dealing with student affairs, with considerable emphasis given to articles dealing with either women students in high schools and colleges or issues and concerns of women student affairs professionals. Subscriptions are included in membership in the National Association for Women Deans, Administrators, and Counselors.

3   *NASPA Journal.* Published four times a year by the National Association of Student Personnel Administrators, 1700 Eighteenth Street, NW, Suite 301, Washington, D.C. 20009.

This journal is published for student affairs professionals holding leadership positions on college and university campuses. The articles stress administrative or programmatic implications of theoretical articles or research reports.

Within the more general field of higher education there are also several generalist publications that often include articles relevant to those in student affairs. These publications include:

4   *AAHE Bulletin* (formerly *College and University Bulletin).* Published ten times a year by the American Association for Higher Education, One Dupont Circle, Suite 780, Washington, D.C. 20036.

This periodical includes short essays, points of view, and interviews regarding current issues and trends in higher education, along with association announcements. Subscription is included with American Association for Higher Education Association membership.

5   *Change: The Magazine of Higher Learning.* Published bi-
      monthly by Heldref Publications, 4000 Albemarle Street
      NW, Washington, D.C. 20016.

This magazine contains news items, perspectives, and feature
articles on subjects related to higher education.

6   *Chronicle of Higher Education.* Forty-eight issues per year,
      published by the Chronicle of Higher Education, Inc.,
      1255 Twenty-Third Street NW, Washington, D.C.
      20037.

This newspaper of higher education provides articles dealing
with problems, concerns, survey results, and current news of
interest to those in higher education. A substantial portion of
each issue contains notices of openings for academic and administrative positions on college and university campuses.

7   *Educational Record: The Magazine of Higher Education.* Pub-
      lished quarterly by the American Council on Education,
      One Dupont Circle, Washington, D.C. 20036.

This magazine publishes articles that deal with a broad range
of issues, concerns, and problems affecting colleges and universities.

8   *Higher Education Abstracts* (formerly *College Student Person-
      nel Abstracts*). Published quarterly by the Claremont
      Graduate School, 740 North College Avenue, Clare-
      mont, Calif. 91711.

This periodical contains brief one-paragraph abstracts of books
and articles dealing with current theory and research on students,
faculty, administrators, and their functions.

9   *Journal of Higher Education.* Published bimonthly by the Ohio State University Press in affiliation with the American Association for Higher Education. Ohio State University Press, 1050 Carmack Road, Columbus, Ohio 43210.

This journal publishes essays, points of views, historical articles, and research reports on a wide variety of subjects dealing with higher education. Reviews of books about higher education are also included.

10   *Review of Higher Education.* Published quarterly by the Association for the Study of Higher Education, President's Building, American University, Washington, D.C. 20016.

This journal contains articles, essays, research, and reviews dealing with the study of higher education. The essays and articles published represent a variety of viewpoints. Subscriptions are included in Association for the Study of Higher Education membership.

References

Cohen, M., and Hale, D. (eds.). *The New Student Left: An Anthology.* Boston: Beacon Press, 1966.

Fitzgerald, L. E., Johnson, W. F., and Norris, W. (eds.). *College Student Personnel.* Boston: Houghton Mifflin, 1970.

Hawkes, H., and Hawkes, A. *Through a Dean's Open Door.* New York: McGraw-Hill, 1945.

Lipset, S., and Wolin, S. (eds.). *The Berkeley Student Revolt: Facts and Interpretations.* New York: Doubleday, 1965.

Mueller, K. H. *Student Personnel Work in Higher Education.* Boston: Houghton Mifflin, 1961.

Williamson, E. G. *How to Counsel Students.* New York: McGraw-Hill, 1939.

Williamson, E. G., and Foley, J. D. *Counseling and Discipline.* New York: McGraw-Hill, 1949.

Wrenn, C. G. *Student Personnel Work in College.* New York: Ronald Press, 1951.

2

Growth of the Student Services Profession

Historically the profession has been identified by the term *college student personnel,* but more recently the field has been labeled *student services* or *student affairs.* Now with the emphasis on the total development of students, the term *student development professional* is becoming increasingly common. The profession comprises college and university staff members who work cooperatively and collaboratively with students, faculty, and administrators to develop approaches that foster human development. These professionals carry out their work with students through formal and informal contacts and relationships, and various titles are given to particular specialists in the field (Fenske, 1989, no. 13).

The profession originally developed from the traditional commitment of American higher education to foster the development of students outside the classroom and laboratory. Prior to the twentieth century these roles were assumed by others, primarily faculty, but beginning in the late 1940s the field began to emerge as a profession. It is a profession in which knowledge gained through research in such disciplines as psychology, sociology, and communications is applied to assist students in their growth and development.

The early emphasis on discipline, morals, and character development has now shifted to activities outside the classroom and more recently to a curricula- and cocurricula-based focus on human growth and development. Various authors have described many different roles for student services professionals, including those of counselor, administrator, teacher, adviser, consultant, behavioral scientist, advocate, researcher, diagnostician, and change agent.

One of the problems facing the student services field as an organized profession is that no specific type of training or degree is required for entry into all or any of the specialties. While a master's degree is required and a Ph.D. often preferred for most positions in college counseling centers, persons obtain entry-level positions in admissions, financial aid, residence life, student activities, and placement with a bachelor's degree in almost any undergraduate field. Many then proceed to complete a master's degree in a student affairs graduate program and even a Ph.D. if they intend to remain in the field and move up the career ladder. Others begin their graduate work immediately following their undergraduate degree and obtain positions in the field after having completed their graduate work. The Ph.D. has become a prerequisite for most top-level student affairs positions in major universities and is becoming increasingly common for the top administrative positions in student affairs in other institutions.

The field has moved from such generalist functions as dean of men and dean of women to numerous specialized agencies on the college campus. Many of these specialties have become professional areas within themselves. The question of how specialized versus how general the training a person entering the field should receive has been discussed at considerable length in the literature. The problems and conflicts facing the field have obviously affected the types of training that prospective professionals receive. Diverging points of view regarding this training also appear in the literature. To what extent should preparation be broad in scope and include courses in basic academic areas, and to what extent should it include specific applied courses in the student affairs field having direct relevance and usefulness in day-to-day work activities in the field? To what extent should training be theoretical and didactic, and to what extent should it include applied courses including practicum and internship experiences?

The question regarding the importance of the role of counseling and how much training in counseling should be included in the preparation of student affairs professionals is also discussed. Certain authors feel that training in counseling is basic while others would downplay or ignore such training, choosing to concentrate on the more administrative and management aspects of the field. One author will argue that training in administration, group dynamics, and budgeting is important in administrative positions in the field and training in counseling is not only irrelevant but actually inhibiting because of the kinds of decisions and administrative policies with which student services administrators must deal. On the other hand, others argue that it is within student affairs that students are treated as individuals — as whole persons — and the training obtained in counseling courses should be the basis of preparation and in fact represents the foundation from which the student affairs field originally emerged. It is in the literature dealing with professional roles that many of these questions are raised and in which answers to at least some of them are suggested.

Students entering the field come from a wide variety of undergraduate programs, with psychology, sociology, and education as the most popular. While obtaining their graduate training, most students in the field hold assistantships in one of the various student services on the campus that provide valuable professional experience and financial support. The most common location for these assistantships is within the residence halls — usually live-in positions that provide room and board but with a reduced stipend.

Student services emerged mostly by default, taking over responsibilities and tasks that were abandoned by faculty and other administrators. It has never developed into a distinct profession for a number of reasons, in part due to the widely varying and far-flung roles held by staff members in the various student services. To a considerable extent the various roles within student services developed because faculty involvement in the development of the whole student declined as emphasis on the research and knowledge-transmitting functions increased. The result has been the development of a number of student personnel specialists working in a highly diversified field of student-related activities.

The history of professional organizations in the field is one of increasing specialization and fragmentation. In earlier days there were five professional groups: the deans of women, the deans of men, the counselors, the registrars and admissions officers, and the placement officers. Now the National Association for Women Deans, Administrators, and Counselors (NAWDAC) represents women in many student affairs positions. The deans of men have become the National Association of Student Personnel Administrators (NASPA), which welcomes those of both sexes and at all levels of student affairs into membership. The counselors have become the American College Personnel Association (ACPA), a division of the American Association for Counseling and Development (AACD). Within ACPA a number of interest groups (called commissions) represent approximately fifteen of the specialties within student services. In a number of cases groups that begin as interest areas within ACPA have now developed into full-fledged professional organizations to which most professionals in that specialty belong. Few in such fields as financial aids and international education have continued to also remain in ACPA.

The admissions counselors have established their own organization — the National Association of College Admissions Counselors (NACAC) — although many also remain with the registrars in the American Association of Collegiate Registrars and Admissions Officers (AACRAO). Among the specialty fields within student services, certain of them have established strong national professional associations, such as those in financial aid, the National Association of Student Financial Aid Administrators (NASFAA); those in placement, the College Placement Council (CPC); and those in college unions, the Association of College Unions-International (ACU-I). Other specialty groups have established national associations that are gaining substantial strength — such as those in international student services, the

National Association for Foreign Student Affairs (NAFSA); and in student residences, the Association of College and University Housing Officers-International (ACUHO-I) — while those in such fields as orientation and student activities are just beginning to form professional associations. As they grow they hold larger conventions, produce more literature related to their field, develop their own codes of ethics, and begin to establish their own standards for employment in the field. Persons in the field develop their primary associations in the field and become less likely to affiliate with one of the three (ACPA, NASPA, and NAWDAC) generalist associations. Increasing specialization thus leads to increasing fragmentation and isolation of professionals in the various student services areas, and the literature in the field increasingly reflects this specialization.

The field, however, is not without at least a few unifying influences. The first two American Council on Education statements of the "student personnel point of view" stated a philosophy that had a unifying effect, and it is expected that the most recent statement will also have some impact (see no. 14). Each of these documents places considerable emphasis on students as individuals and as whole persons, with a number of different functions identified as responsibilities of professionals in this field. The concept of student development that emphasizes developmental tasks, stages, and developmental growth is having a substantial effect on the way that those in the field view their work with students. The student development theories developed by theorists such as Perry (1981, no. 56) and Chickering (1969, no. 45) have not only had an effect upon the conceptualization of the field but have had a particularly strong impact on the preparation programs. At present almost all graduates of such programs have studied a number of such theories, and they have become the basis around which much of their academic program has revolved. The concept of student development is now well accepted by many professionals in various specialized areas. One of the major current issues for these professionals is their attempt to apply developmental theories to their day-by-day practice.

During the 1970s and up to the present, the movement

has been away from controlling student behavior and attempting to provide services that make educational and developmental contributions to students. The emphasis has been a holistic view, recognizing stages and transitions through which college-aged students pass.

A recent professional development in the field has been the creation of a set of standards and guidelines for student services/development programs by the Council for the Advancement of Standards (CAS). These have been developed by representatives of most of the professional associations for sixteen of the functional areas within student services, along with a separate set of standards for preparation programs. With the exception of those developed for preparation programs, the standards have no official accrediting body, but they allow professionals in each of the areas to evaluate the programs for which they are responsible on their own campus. They also provide a set of guidelines for both external accrediting agencies and internal review committees in their examination of student services programs. As such, they are likely to have a considerable impact on student affairs programs on the nation's campuses.

The unique philosophy of student personnel work and the various roles that professionals in this field can assume has been the subject of numerous articles and books since the emergence of full-time student services personnel. To be truly well read in this area requires going back in the literature and into the history of the field to the publications from its beginnings — not just the literature reviewed in this volume, which covers only the more recent years. The professional literature deals with not only questions regarding theories, roles, and philosophies of student affairs work but also how these theories and philosophies can be applied by practitioners in their work on college and university campuses. It is not just a question of which theories and which philosophies a practitioner chooses to espouse but also how to apply these theories and philosophies in everyday interactions with students.

There are certain resources, some listed here and some from earlier times, that deal with the very real question of the extent to which the field has become a "true" profession. There are also articles and chapters dealing with ethics in the field, the extent to which the field has a research base, and surveys of career patterns and career ladders — all of which are important to the field, particularly as it perceives itself and is perceived by others to have achieved the status of an established profession.

History of the Field

★ 11   Belson, Beverly A., and Fitzgerald, Laurine E. (ed.). *Thus, We Spoke. ACPA-NAWDAC, 1958–1975.* Carbondale, Ill.: American College Personnel Association, Southern Illinois University Press, 1983. 256 pages.

This edited volume consists of articles written by leaders in the college student personnel field over a period of twenty-two years. They were originally published in either the *Journal of College Student Personnel* or the *Journal of the National Association for Women Deans, Administrators, and Counselors.* The articles generally deal with three topics — needs of students on the college campus, the college student personnel profession, and the student personnel professional organizations.

★ 12   Belson, Beverly, and Stamatakos, Louis (eds.). *The Student Affairs Profession: A Selected Bibliography.* (2nd ed.) Alexandria, Va.: American College Personnel Association, 1988. 203 pages.

This edited volume includes historical and philosophical selections covering forty student affairs topics. The selections include planning, organization, administration, and a variety of other specific functions and topics within student affairs. Appendixes list ACPA publications, basic test books, and periodicals.

13   Fenske, Robert H. "Historical Foundations of Student
      Services." In Ursula Delworth, Gary Hanson, and Asso-
      ciates, *Student Services: A Handbook for the Profession.* (2nd
      ed.) San Francisco: Jossey-Bass, 1989, pp. 5–24.

The author briefly describes the history of higher education in
this country with particular emphasis on the concern of institutions for the character development of students. He traces the
change from institutions supported by religious denominations,
with their concerns about the piety of their students and their
desire for control over students' lives, to the secularization of
most of today's higher education. He also discusses the trend
in the role of faculty from total involvement in the student service functions to almost total detachment. For a description of
Delworth and Hanson's complete work see entry no. 23.

★14   National Association of Student Personnel Administra-
      tors. *Points of View.* Washington, D.C.: National Associa-
      tion of Student Personnel Administrators, 1989. 64
      pages.

This anthology contains the three primary historical documents
of the student affairs profession: *The Student Personnel Point of View,
1937; The Student Personnel Point of View, 1949;* and *A Perspective
on Student Affairs, 1987.* These three references include many of
the assumptions and beliefs that shape the student affairs field.
They also include the origin of the term *student personnel* and point
out the necessity of considering the whole student in postsecondary education.

★15   Saddlemire, Gerald L., and Rentz, Audrey L. (eds.).
      Student Affairs — A Profession's Heritage. Carbondale, Ill.:
      American College Personnel Association, Southern Il-
      linois University Press, 1986. 439 pages.

This edited volume attempts to preserve the legacy of the student affairs profession through a compilation of papers, articles,
speeches, and statements gathered from a variety of sources.
The volume gathers together in one source a group of signif-

icant, but often difficult to locate, articles and documents. The progress of the professional field can be discerned from the issues and predictions covered in these documents, which also include the two original American Council on Education "Student Personnel Points of View."

Philosophy and Concerns

16   American College Testing Program. *Toward the Future Vitality of Student Development Services.* Iowa City, Iowa: American College Testing Program, 1985. 40 pages.

This report was developed for student development professionals in community colleges. The first three chapters examine the student development philosophy on two-year campuses and effective leadership in student services. The fourth and final chapter is composed of the well-known 1984 Traverse City Statement entitled "Toward the Future Vitality of Student Development Services."

17   Brown, Robert D. *Student Development in Tomorrow's Higher Education: A Return to the Academy.* Alexandria, Va.: American College Personnel Association, no. 16, 1972. 55 pages.

A discussion of the future of student services in higher education, this monograph is of particular historical importance due to its focus on the philosophy and roles of the student services professional. It describes how to make use of student development concepts to "return to the academy" and become more integrated with the academic mission of the institution.

18   Canon, Harry J. "Developmental Tasks for the Profession: The Next Twenty-Five Years." *Journal of College Student Personnel,* 1984, *2,* 105–111.

A set of objectives for the student personnel profession, and for the American College Personnel Association specifically, is discussed in terms of advancing theory, professional roles, and campus support.

19   Canon, Harry J., and Brown, Robert D. (eds.). *Applied Ethics in Student Services*. New Directions in Student Services, no. 30. San Francisco: Jossey-Bass, 1985. 106 pages.

With the assumption that maintenance of an ethical climate is a necessary precondition for accomplishment of developmental tasks, this volume explores ethics in student affairs. Ethical problems from daily practice and the development of an ethical community are part of the discussion that seeks to encourage the examination of ethics in the student services profession.

20   Garland, Peter H. *Serving More than Students: A Critical Need for College Student Personnel Services*. Washington, D.C.: Association for the Study of Higher Education, 1985. 143 pages.

The evolution of student affairs is presented. Garland describes the increasingly complex set of duties being added to the ever evolving roles of student affairs professionals. The impact of trends in higher education, such as the decreasing birth rate, growth of minority populations, changing financial conditions, and changing student values and needs are discussed and related to future professional roles.

21   Stamatakos, Louis C., and Rogers, Russell R. "Student Affairs: A Profession in Need of a Philosophy." *Journal of College Student Personnel*, 1984, *25*, 400–411.

This article is an exploration of the nature and scope of the student affairs profession's philosophy and the documents that present the student personnel point of view. The values, role, and functions based on this philosophy and the professional identity that results are included in this discussion.

General Resources in the Field

22 Bradley, Russell K.; Coomes, Michael D.; and Kuh, George D. "A Typology for Classifying Student Affairs Knowledge." *Journal of College Student Personnel,* 1985, *26,* 11–18.

This article contains six categories used to classify student affairs knowledge as a way of categorizing student affairs literature. The rationale for devising such a typology and its usefulness are discussed.

★23 Delworth, Ursula; Hanson, Gary R.; and Associates. *Student Services: A Handbook for the Profession.* (2nd ed.) San Francisco: Jossey-Bass, 1989. 665 pages.

This edited book contains twenty-four chapters by student affairs professionals that cut across many aspects of the student services profession. The volume is designed primarily for graduate student courses and entry-level practitioners but still contains much useful information for student services professionals as they attempt to plan, deliver, and evaluate student services programs. The volume is divided into six major sections that define the structure of the student services profession: (1) professional roots and commitments, (2) theoretical bases of the profession, (3) roles and models for practice, (4) essential competencies and techniques, (5) organizing and managing programs and services, and (6) emerging roles and opportunities. This book is currently the primary resource for an introduction to the student services field and is a popular graduate student text.

24 Eddy, John; Dameron, Joseph D.; and Borland, David T. (eds.). *College Student Personnel Development, Administration, and Counseling.* (2nd ed.) Lanham, Md.: University Press of America, 1980. 538 pages.

This book provides an overview of the professional field of college student personnel work. Fifty-four chapters cover historical, legal, organizational, administrative, and future developments. A sample literature review, organizational glossary, professional organization listing, and suggested readings are also included. The significance and quality of the chapters varies considerably, making this an inconsistent resource.

25 Harrington, Thomas F. (ed.). *Student Personnel Work in Urban Colleges.* New York: Intext, 1974. 328 pages.

Although supposedly aimed primarily at those in urban institutions, this edited text actually contains chapters dealing with a wide variety of subjects by a number of different authors. Several chapters deal with the role of student personnel work on the campus. Others deal with legal issues, student values, and problems of the commuter student.

★26 Owens, Hilda F.; Witten, Charles H.; and Bailey, Walter R. (eds.). *College Student Personnel Administration: An Anthology.* Springfield, Ill.: Thomas, 1982. 391 pages.

This book of readings generally focuses on significant topics in the administration of college student personnel services. Included are readings dealing with the history, functions, and development of the student affairs profession. Other readings deal with the organization and administration of student services, and three selections deal with legal issues.

★27 Packwood, William T. (ed.). *College Student Personnel Services.* Springfield, Ill.: Thomas, 1977. 530 pages.

Each of the chapters in this volume summarizes research studies that have been conducted in each of fourteen different student services ranging from admissions through financial aid, student activities, counseling, and graduation. The summaries of studies in each of the services have made this volume a basic text in many graduate courses that introduce graduate students to the field of student services in higher education. However, the research summaries are now becoming dated.

Career Patterns

28   Farley, Jennie. *Academic Women and Employment Discrimination: A Critical Annotated Bibliography.* Ithaca, N.Y.: Cornell University, 1982. 103 pages.

This bibliography addresses sex discrimination in higher education and efforts to eliminate it. The majority of sources cited are professional journals from such disciplines as law, sociology, psychology, education, and business. Policy statements and recommendations from commissions and associations are also included.

29   Gelwick, Beverly Prosser (ed.). *Up the Ladder: Women, Professionals, and Clients in College Student Personnel.* Alexandria, Va.: American College Personnel Association, 1979. 136 pages.

This volume, geared toward women in the student affairs profession, presents articles designed to help women advance their status within the field through publishing and improved administrative and consulting skills.

30   Harder, Martha B. "Career Patterns of Chief Student Personnel Administrators." *Journal of College Student Personnel,* 1983, *24,* 443–448.

This article is a survey of the educational preparation, professional experiences, and career patterns of 104 chief student personnel administrators in the southeastern United States.

31   Kirby, Alan F., and Woodward, Dudley (eds.). *Career Perspectives in Student Affairs.* Columbus, Ohio: National Association of Student Personnel Administrators, 1984. 76 pages.

This is a monograph presenting a broad overview of career-related issues in student affairs, with chapters written by several prominent practitioners and educators.

32   Ostroth, D. David, Efird, Frances D., and Lerman, Lewis S. "Career Patterns of Chief Student Affairs Officers." *Journal of College Student Personnel,* 1984, *25,* 443–448.

This article contains the results of a survey on the careers of a national sample of chief student affairs officers. Included in the survey were their educational backgrounds, professional activities, work experiences, career aspirations, and current and past positions. It suggests that mobility among and into chief student affairs positions appears to have been decreasing in recent years.

33   Rentz, Audrey L., and Knock, Gary H. *Careers in the College Student Personnel Profession.* Alexandria, Va.: American Association for Counseling and Development, 1987. 16 pages.

This brief publication is intended for those considering entering the field of college student affairs. The various roles and functions in the field are briefly described, along with the types of professional preparation needed and the career ladder in the field.

34   Tinsley, Adrian; Secor, Cynthia; and Kaplan, Sheila (eds.). *Women in Higher Education Administration.* New Directions for Higher Education, no. 45. San Francisco: Jossey-Bass, 1984. 96 pages.

This publication explores the professional development process of women in higher education administration, including personal and institutional obstacles, assessment of approaches for fostering administrative advancement, and how institutions can actively seek out women administrators.

Professional Preparation

★35 Knock, Gary H. *Perspectives on the Preparation of Student Affairs Professionals.* Alexandria, Va.: American College Personnel Association, 1977. 177 pages.

This edited collection of articles explores the components of student personnel preparation programs. Systems approaches, experiential learning, social intervention, and the needs of community college professionals are examples of the types of issues included. As many of these issues are still being addressed in preparation programs today, this continues to be a relevant resource.

36 Moore, Leila V., and Young, Robert T. (eds.). *Expanding Opportunities for Professional Education.* New Directions for Student Services, no. 37. San Francisco: Jossey-Bass, 1987. 83 pages.

A comprehensive model to determine the professional education needs of staff members is presented. The authors also examine ways to enhance professional development, thereby increasing job satisfaction and mobility, and promoting retention.

Status as a Profession

★37 Stamatakos, Louis C. "Student Affairs Progress Toward Professionalism: Recommendations for Action. Part I." *Journal of College Student Personnel,* 1981, *22,* 105–112.

In this article the author reviews the various criteria for the establishment of a profession and examines the extent to which college student affairs has reached professional status. The three criteria discussed in this article are the self-imposition of standards, the definition of job functions and titles, and the possession of specialized knowledge and skills.

★38 Stamatakos, Louis C. "Student Affairs Progress Toward Professionalism: Recommendations for Action. Part II." *Journal of College Student Personnel*, 1981, *22*, 197–207.

This is the second part of an analysis to determine the extent to which student affairs personnel have progressed in meeting the various criteria of a recognized profession. This part deals with the varying legal recognition, the development of ethics, and the application of standards of selection and training.

Relevant Issues in Higher Education

39 Henderson, Algo D., and Henderson, Jean Glidden. *Higher Education in America: Problems, Priorities, and Prospects.* San Francisco: Jossey-Bass, 1974. 282 pages.

A survey introduction to higher education in its many forms, including community colleges, liberal arts colleges and universities, and professional schools, this volume considers issues ranging from academic freedom to students, curriculum, and finance.

40 Henry, David D. *Challenges Past, Challenges Present: An Analysis of American Higher Education Since 1930.* San Francisco: Jossey-Bass, 1975. 173 pages.

This essay, written for the Carnegie Council on Policy Studies, highlights the changes that occurred in American higher education during the period between 1930 and 1970 and discusses trends and problems that can be expected in the future.

★41 Martin, Warren B. *A College of Character: Renewing the Purpose and Content of College Education.* San Francisco: Jossey-Bass, 1982. 215 pages.

This publication, commissioned by the American Council on Education, won a 1982–1983 award from the Association of American Colleges for being the most significant contribution to studies on liberal education for that year. It includes an examination of the major issues confronting undergraduate education, what roles colleges should be striving toward, and what characteristics distinguish a particular college from other institutions.

Professional Newsletters

42 *ACPA Developments.* Published quarterly by the American College Personnel Association, 2 Skyline Place, Suite 400, 5203 Leesburg Pike, Falls Church, Va. 22041.

This quarterly newsletter for American College Personnel Association members describes the activities of the association and contains several articles examining issues in the field.

43 *NASPA Forum.* Published eight times a year by the National Association of Student Personnel Administrators, 1700 Eighteenth Street NW, Suite 301, Washington, D.C. 20009.

This newsletter contains announcements of the Association of Student Personnel Administrators and one or two articles dealing with student personnel issues.

3

Student Characteristics
and Development

Characteristics of students and how they change during the college years represent extremely important areas of knowledge that define the unique mission of student services professionals. Recently this knowledge has included theoretical and empirical information on the developmental changes that typically occur among students during the college years. Many decisions made in higher education regarding admissions, curriculum changes, and student services policies should be made only after taking this knowledge into consideration.

The literature regarding college students began to grow rapidly during the 1950s and early 1960s. It continued to grow during the late 1960s and early 1970s, but much of it during this period concentrated on various aspects of student activism and characteristics of activist students. During the late 1970s and 1980s the focus shifted to research related to a variety of aspects and characteristics of college students. During the last decade much of this literature has concentrated on student development theory and the developmental changes that occur during the undergraduate years.

With the decline of the *in loco parentis* attitudes on the part of higher education administrators, many rules, strict codes of conduct, and women's residence hall regulations were eliminated. Encouraging and affecting the development of the whole person, a fundamental goal expressed by most colleges and universities in their catalogues, became the primary mission of many in the student services field. The result was a heightened interest in theories and research dealing with student development, and much of the current research and writing in the field is related to these concepts.

Theories of student development have appeared that emphasize different aspects of development, including psychosocial development; cognitive development; moral, ethical, and values development; ego development; and the impact of the environment on development. Books and articles setting forth these theories began to appear in the 1970s and have continued to the present.

One of the earliest conceptualizations of student development is Nevitt Sanford's (1962, no. 87) psychosocial theory that attempted to relate personality development to the university curriculum. Similar to Sanford's theory with its basis in Freudian psychology, Arthur Chickering's (1969, no. 45) vectors of development also build on the psychoanalytic tradition. Specifically, Chickering's model is an elaboration of Erik Erikson's stages of identity and intimacy. Chickering's model of student development focuses on the particular developmental concerns of students relevant to the social situation they find themselves in during their years at the university.

In contrast to this, Lawrence Kohlberg's (1981, no. 49) cognitive development theory of moral reasoning built on the ideas of Jean Piaget. This theory holds that the stages of moral development are universal and determined from one another by how and why judgments are made. While Kohlberg's work is aimed at the population in general, William Perry's (1981, no. 56) model is a cognitive developmental scheme of positions of intellectual development specifically aimed at the university years. He has formulated a nine-position scheme that outlines the evolution in students' thinking about the nature of knowledge, truth, and values and the meaning of life and responsibilities. Gilligan (1982, no. 46) suggested differing male and female approaches and Loevinger (see entry 52) originally developed her milestones of ego development for women.

Distinct from these conceptualizations of college student

development is Douglas Heath's (see entry 47) *Model of Psychological Maturity.* This model represents an attempt to empirically define maturity and develop a theory that describes the nature of maturing and the psychological functions and processes characteristic of a mature person.

In addition, new approaches in programs designed to bring about desired development were initiated on many campuses, and publications describing these applications of the theories have appeared during the last decade. In some cases these approaches have been new and innovative in nature, but in many instances they have merely represented traditional activities and programs under a different label.

After different models and programs have been established to assist students to develop along the lines of a particular theory, the next problem, of course, is to measure or evaluate the effects or the impact of such activities on the development of students. The need, therefore, has arisen to measure such impact, if any, and to accomplish this, it has been necessary to attempt to develop procedures and instruments that can adequately measure development. Several resources that describe methods of assessing student development, including reliable and valid measurement instruments, are referenced in this chapter. The general area of assessment of student development and the evaluation of various programs is one in which much research and development is still needed.

The first three sections of this chapter address resources describing various theories of student development, followed by those describing various applications and models of student development theory, and then lastly, those dealing with the assessment of student development.

For a much longer period, a large number of characteristics of college students have been studied and described. The book *The American College,* edited by Nevitt Sanford (no. 87) in 1962 represented an early attempt to summarize research and knowledge then available about college students.

Alexander Astin (1977, no. 90, and 1987, no. 91) has a long history of studying college students and in recent years has conducted annual surveys that have produced considerable information about them. A 1977 book by Bowen (no. 83) summarized much of the knowledge of the impact of higher education upon students at the time that his book appeared.

The emphasis on student development, which has been focused primarily upon traditionally aged majority students, has now begun to focus on such groups as minorities, adults, and other nontraditionally aged students. In addition, Cross (1971, no. 398) has discussed the development of a new group of students on the campus — those who are underprepared, lack academic skills, and are not motivated toward academic goals. Several of the resources included here deal with the general problem of relating student development theory to actual practice in student services agencies. The difficulty of translating theory to practice is one felt by most practitioners, not only in dealing with minorities and nontraditional students but in their work with typical majority students as well. It is expected that literature in the form of both books and journal articles will continue to be produced that will address this issue.

Student Development Theory

44 Caple, Richard B. "The Change Process in Developmental Theory: A Self-Organization Paradigm. Part I and II." *Journal of College Student Personnel,* 1987, *28,* 4–11, 100–104.

Utilizing self-organization theory as compared with other typical student development theories, the author makes the case for the need for challenge and disequilibrium on the campus to bring about major change and growth among individual students. These articles are followed by commentaries from seven different authorities in the field.

★45   Chickering, Arthur W. *Education and Identity*. San Francisco: Jossey-Bass, 1969. 367 pages.

In this volume the author presents his seven-vector theory regarding the psychosocial development of college students. This theory has had a profound impact on the student services field. Institutional environments and practices that affect student development on these dimensions are discussed, along with recommendations for change.

46   Gilligan, Carol. *In a Different Voice: Psychological Theory and Women's Development*. Cambridge, MA: Harvard University Press, 1982. 184 pages.

In this book the author describes her revision of Kohlberg's principles of moral development which she feels contain a masculine bias. She presents evidence that women's conceptions of morality place greater emphasis upon interpersonal relationships and obligations.

47   Heath, Douglas H. *Growing Up in College: Liberal Education and Maturity*. San Francisco: Jossey-Bass, 1968. 326 pages.

In this volume the author reports the results of his research on student development that he conducted in the United States and in several other countries. He sets forth his four dimensions of maturity. His theory of development represents an important conception of college and university student development.

48   Knefelkamp, Lee; Widick, Carole; and Parker, Clyde A. (eds.). *Applying New Developmental Findings*. New Directions for Student Services, no. 4. San Francisco: Jossey-Bass, 1978. 125 pages.

This sourcebook is an excellent overview of cognitive and social-emotional developmental theories of the college years. While it includes an exploration of how these theories can be applied to student services practice, its primary strength lies in providing

a concise description of the major theories in the student development field.

49 Kohlberg, Lawrence. *The Philosophy of Moral Development:
Moral Stages and the Idea of Justice.* San Francisco: Harper
& Row, 1981. 441 pages.

This book consists of ten essays in which the author applies his
theory of moral development to the aims of education, the idea
of justice, and legal and political issues. One of the essays deals
with the question of a possible seventh stage, and a summary
of the six stages is presented in the appendix.

★50 Kohlberg, Lawrence. *The Psychology of Moral Development:
The Nature and Validity of Moral Stages.* San Francisco:
Harper & Row, 1984. 729 pages.

This volume summarizes the current formulation of Kohlberg's
stages of moral development. It includes an outline of the various
stages and ideas of justice that are found within them, and
describes the theoretical foundations of moral development. The
dilemmas presented in the interviews with which moral development is measured are described.

51 Kuh, George D.; Whitt, Elizabeth J.; and Shedd, Jill
D. *Student Affairs 2001: A Paradigmatic Odyssey.* Alexandria, Va.: American College Personnel Association,
1987. 137 pages.

In this monograph the authors reexamine certain of the assumptions in student affairs and suggest that student development
and change in organizations are unpredictable rather than orderly
and cumulative. The implications of this alternative view for
student affairs are then explored.

52 Loevinger, Jane. *Ego Development: Conceptions and Theories.*
San Francisco: Jossey-Bass, 1976. 504 pages.

In this volume the author sets forth her theory of ego development consisting of six stages with several transitional points between stages. She also presents some alternative conceptions,

and traces the history of the concept of the ego. Research related to ego development is reviewed and various attempts to assess ego development are discussed.

★53   Morrill, Weston H.; Hurst, James C.; and Oetting, E. R. (eds.) *Dimensions of Intervention for Student Development.* New York: Wiley, 1980. 339 pages.

This book provides a model of a conceptual framework of student affairs work as a professional field in which professionals are knowledgeable experts on students and campus environments and are thus able to provide interventions that promote student development. The framework includes a three-dimensional model designed to integrate the various theories of student development into one general approach. The last section of the book presents examples in which this framework has been utilized in a number of student services functional areas.

54   Parker, Clyde A. (ed.). *Encouraging Development in College Students.* Minneapolis: University of Minnesota Press, 1978. 295 pages.

This is a compilation of papers from a conference in which various theories of college student development were presented, discussed, and critiqued. The chapters emphasize reactions to the theories and their implications for practice rather than a detailed presentation of the theories themselves, which have been outlined in greater detail in other publications.

55   Pascarella, Ernest T. "College Environmental Influences on Learning and Cognitive Development: A Critical Review and Synthesis." In John C. Smart (ed.), *Higher Education: Handbook of Theory and Research.* Vol. 1. New York: Agathon Press, 1985, pp. 1–61.

In this chapter the author reviews the evidence of growth in cognitive development in college and the effect of different institutions and different college experiences on this development.

56 Perry, William G., Jr. "Cognitive and Ethical Growth: The Making of Meaning." In Arthur W. Chickering and Associates, *The Modern American College: Responding to the New Realities of Diverse Students and a Changing Society.* San Francisco: Jossey-Bass, 1981, pp. 76–116.

The author has developed a theory of stages of cognitive and ethical growth that emphasizes the development of these concepts during the college years. In this chapter he presents some of his more recent thinking regarding the hierarchy of stages, from dualism through relativism to commitment within relativism. For a description of Chickering's complete work see entry no. 85.

57 Rich, John M., and DeVitis, Joseph L. *Theories of Moral Development.* Springfield, Ill.: Thomas, 1985. 138 pages.

In this book certain cognitive and psychosocial theories dealing with moral development are summarized and organized according to the chronological ages to which they apply.

58 Rodgers, Robert F. "Student Development." In Ursula Delworth, Gary R. Hanson, and Associates, *Student Services: A Handbook for the Profession.* (2nd ed.) San Francisco: Jossey-Bass, 1989, pp. 117–164.

In this chapter the author briefly describes several theories of college student development. He organizes the theories into four types — psychosocial, cognitive-structural, typological, and person-environment interaction. Developmental theories within each of the first three types are discussed and compared. (Person-environment interaction theories are covered in another chapter in this volume.) For a description of Delworth and Hanson's complete work see entry no. 23.

Applications of Student Development Theory

59   Ahrendt, Kenneth M. (ed.). *Teaching the Developmental Education Student*. New Directions for Community Colleges, no. 57. San Francisco: Jossey-Bass, 1987. 116 pages.

An explanation of how developmental education can be integrated throughout the curriculum, this volume addresses ways of responding to criticisms of developmental education as well as specific recommendations for different students and curricula.

60   Barrow, John C. *Fostering Cognitive Development of Students: A New Approach to Counseling and Program Planning*. San Francisco: Jossey-Bass, 1986. 392 pages.

This volume presents ways in which cognitive development theories and models can be effectively used in counseling college students. It includes suggestions for setting up individual and group interventions, as well as outreach programs. Applications and case studies to meet a variety of different developmental needs of students are presented for use in individual counseling as well as in workshops.

★61   Creamer, Don G. (ed.). *Student Development in Higher Education: Theories, Practices, and Future Directions*. Washington, D.C.: American College Personnel Association, 1980. 312 pages.

This edited volume contains an outstanding comprehensive summary of the theories underlying college student development, followed by chapters dealing with considerations, strategies, and programs designed to encourage student development and the obstacles that operate against such programs.

62   Creamer, Don G., and Dassance, Charles R. (eds.). *Opportunities for Student Development in Two-Year Colleges*. Washington, D.C.: National Association of Student Personnel Administrators, 1986. 87 pages.

This edited monograph presents the challenges, opportunities, and problems encountered in attempting to establish programs designed to promote student development in two-year colleges. Chapters deal with the history and mission of two-year colleges, the diverse student population, and current and future challenges for the institutions and their student affairs staffs to achieve student development goals.

63   Drew, David E. (ed.). *Increasing Student Development Options in College.* New Directions for Education and Work, no. 4. San Francisco: Jossey-Bass, 1978. 106 pages.

A consideration of college as an opportunity for more than cognitive growth and development is presented. Contributions from leading researchers focus on the ways in which institutions can have an impact on the life roles of students in a meaningful and constructive fashion.

64   Fried, Jane (ed.). *Education for Student Development.* New Directions for Student Services, no. 15. San Francisco: Jossey-Bass, 1981. 111 pages.

A consideration of life skills and academic skills in the classroom was the impetus for this in-depth look at methods, principles of design, and evaluation for developmental courses. Consultation models, case studies of actual courses, and discussions of academic decision making combine to provide a resource for instruction that integrates both.

65   Johnson, Cynthia S., and Pyle, Richard K. (eds.). *Enhancing Student Development with Computers.* New Directions for Student Services, no. 26. San Francisco: Jossey-Bass, 1984. 106 pages.

This sourcebook describes the current computer programs available to the student affairs professional, including the selection of hardware and software. It discusses how to effectively manage computer resources, general applications for student development, ethical considerations of computer use, and future trends.

66   Loxley, Janet, and Whiteley, John. *Character Development in College Students: The Curriculum and Longitudinal Results.* Vol. 2. Alexandria, Va.: American Association for Counseling and Development, 1986. 367 pages.

This second volume describes a study of and model for character development in higher education. It covers a four-year research experiment in which an extensive psychological and educational intervention was employed with undergraduate students in a university residence hall. The authors contend that character development is a key purpose of higher education and suggest interventions that can be effective with college freshmen. For Volume One see entry no. 71.

67   McBee, M. Louise (ed.). *Rethinking College Responsibilities for Values.* New Directions for Higher Education, no. 31. San Francisco: Jossey-Bass, 1980. 97 pages.

These papers that were delivered at a symposium explore the impact of college on the development of students' ethical values and morals, including a discussion of the controversy over the appropriate role in values education for our institutions.

★68   Miller, Theodore K., and Prince, Judith S. *The Future of Student Affairs: A Guide to Student Development for Tomorrow's Higher Education.* San Francisco: Jossey-Bass, 1976. 220 pages.

This volume, a significant contribution to the student development concept, presents an extension of the American College Personnel Association's Tomorrow's Higher Education (T.H.E.) project. It provides the basic theories of human developmental concepts in higher education, along with the rationale for their use, and then describes techniques, strategies, concepts, and organizational patterns useful in attempting to apply this model.

69 Morrill, Richard L. *Teaching Values in College: Facilitating Development of Ethical, Moral, and Value Awareness in Students.* San Francisco: Jossey-Bass, 1980. 169 pages.

This guide to methods of teaching ethics and values on campus emphasizes a campus-wide program that incorporates minor changes in curriculum and the environment to stimulate the development of moral awareness in students.

70 Newton, Fred B., and Ender, Kenneth L. (eds.). *Student Development Practices: Strategies for Making a Difference.* Springfield, Ill.: Thomas, 1980. 348 pages.

Chapters in this edited volume focus on how student development principles and theories can be transformed into specific strategies in the delivery of student affairs services. Various delivery modes including courses, workshops, programs, and counseling as well as ways to improve overall campus community life are discussed.

71 Whiteley, John M. *Character Development in College Students: The Freshman Year.* Vol. 1. Alexandria, Va.: American Association for Counseling and Development, 1982. 356 pages.

This volume reports the initial phase of a longitudinal study of freshmen volunteers in a year-long residential program with a psychological intervention designed to increase the students' developmental status on the three dimensions of character: moral maturity, principal thinking, and ego development. For Volume Two see entry no. 66.

Assessment of Student Development

72 Baxter-Magolda, Marsha B., and Porterfield, William F. *Assessing Intellectual Development: The Link Between Theory and Practice.* Alexandria, Va.: American College Personnel Association, 1988. 243 pages.

This volume provides information about the Measure of Epistemological Reflection (MER), an instrument designed to provide a measure of intellectual development according to the Perry scheme. The book includes information needed to administer and rate the MER.

73   Braskamp, Larry A. *Spectrum Assessment Surveys for Higher Education Source Book.* Champaign, Ill.: MetriTech Inc., 1988. 36 pages.

This sourcebook describes the instruction and validation of the Spectrum battery of scales that have been developed to assess students' personal incentives and perceptions of the institutional culture. Included are copies of both versions and the faculty/staff and student surveys, each of which contains 200 items grouped into twenty-two different scales or subscales.

74   Ewell, Peter T. (ed.). *Assessing Educational Outcomes.* New Directions for Institutional Research, no. 47. San Francisco: Jossey-Bass, 1985. 128 pages.

A practical, how-to guide for the collection, use, and communication of information regarding the outcomes of college education. Provides descriptions of data-collection techniques and explains how to make decisions about the form and purpose of outcome studies. Case studies are provided to demonstrate how assessment models have been used successfully.

75   Hanson, Gary R. (ed.). *Measuring Student Development.* New Directions for Student Services, no. 20. San Francisco: Jossey-Bass, 1982. 124 pages.

A primary concern of student affairs professionals is the development of students while in college. This volume addresses important components of assessing development, including a rationale for measurement and choosing appropriate instruments. A case study of implementation of assessment results for programming is presented.

76 Hood, Albert B. (ed.). *The Iowa Student Development Inventories.* Iowa City, Iowa: Hitech Press, 1986. 106 pages.

This monograph contains a description of seven standardized instruments designed to measure student development along the different Chickering vectors. A description of the development of each of the seven instruments as well as the inventories themselves, their subscales and scoring keys, and some initial norms are included.

77 Kuh, George D. *Indices of Quality in the Undergraduate Experience.* Washington, D.C.: American Association for Higher Education, 1981. 43 pages.

The need to measure the quality of the undergraduate experience is presented, and several input indices and outcome indices that can be used to assess this quality are suggested.

78 Nucci, Larry, and Pascarella, Ernest T. "The Influence of College on Moral Development." In John C. Smart (ed.), *Higher Education: Handbook of Theory and Research.* Vol. 3. New York: Agathon Press, 1987, pp. 271–326.

The moral development theories of Kohlberg and Perry are discussed along with instruments used to assess moral developments during the college years. Evidence of moral development using these instruments is summarized.

★79 Pace, C. Robert. *Measuring Outcomes of College: Fifty Years of Findings and Recommendations for the Future.* San Francisco: Jossey-Bass, 1979. 188 pages.

This book summarizes the results of almost fifty years of research dealing with achievement testing, student surveys, and alumni studies. These studies have attempted to identify changes that occur during the undergraduate years and measure the effects of the college experience on graduates in their later lives. The results of several major achievement testing programs and the achievement results conducted by large testing agencies are included in this literature review.

80   Winston, Roger B., Jr., and Miller, Theodore K. *Student Developmental Task and Life Inventory Manual.* Athens, Ga.: Student Development Associates, 1987. 47 pages.

This manual presents scoring, interpretation, reliability, and validity information for the Student Development Task and Lifestyle Inventory (SDTLI). The 140-item inventory consists of fourteen scales and subscales that represent behaviors, feelings, and attitudes that students can be expected to demonstrate when they have satisfactorily achieved certain developmental tasks.

College Student General Resources

★81   Astin, Alexander W. *Achieving Educational Excellence: A Critical Assessment of Priorities and Practices in Higher Education.* San Francisco: Jossey-Bass, 1985. 254 pages.

In this underrated volume Astin argues that the development of human talent is the primary objective of higher education and that the current measures of institutional excellence and reputation are unrelated to this primary objective. He prescribes actively involving students in the educational enterprise as the most important ingredient in developing this talent.

82   Baird, Leonard L.; Hartnett, Rodney T.; and Associates. *Understanding Student and Faculty Life.* San Francisco: Jossey-Bass, 1980. 299 pages.

In this volume a number of authors discuss various instruments, variables, and efforts dealing with the description of campus environments and the effects of these environments upon students. Included are chapters describing various surveys and instruments for assessing campus environments, the usefulness of collecting student background data, information systems designed to use such information, and the importance of using such information in formulating and implementing policy.

★83　Bowen, Howard R. *Investment in Learning: The Individual and Social Value of American Higher Education.* San Francisco: Jossey-Bass, 1977. 507 pages.

In this volume the author reviews the literature dealing with the intended goals and outcomes of higher education and the results of many research studies designed to measure development in college and the extent to which expected outcomes are achieved. Although written by an economist who is concerned with the economic value of higher education, both to the individual and to society, literature related to cognitive, emotional, moral, and practical development is also summarized. The book thus provides a useful reference for those concerned with the value of higher education as measured by a wide variety of differing variables.

★84　Boyer, Ernest L. *College: The Undergraduate Experience in America.* New York: Harper & Row, 1987. 328 pages.

This discussion of undergraduate education is based on the findings of an extensive study of twenty-nine campuses and surveys of large numbers of faculty, students, and staff supported by the Carnegie Foundation on the Advancement of Teaching. It calls for the reinstitution of a liberal education core and more emphasis on community service. The central theme of the book is the tension between the individual self-interests of both students and faculty members and the shared concerns of community and society on which most institutions were founded.

★85　Chickering, Arthur W., and Associates. *The Modern American College: Responding to the New Realities of Diverse Students and a Changing Society.* San Francisco: Jossey-Bass, 1981. 810 pages.

This edited volume contains forty-two separate chapters dealing with the diverse needs of students in American higher education. The volume is divided into three parts. The first deals with cognitive and psychosocial theories of student development and the needs of particular groups of students, such as the vocationally undecided, women, minorities, and adult learners. The

second portion contains chapters discussing students and the
curriculum in a number of particular college majors. The third
discusses various instructional strategies in higher education as
well as in various out-of-class experiences.

86   Giroux, Roy F.; Biggs, Donald A.; Hoffman, Alan M.;
      and Pietrofesa, John J. (eds.). *College Student Development
      Revisited: Programs, Issues, and Practices.* Alexandria, Va.:
      American Association for Counseling and Development,
      1979. 364 pages.

This volume contains fifty-nine articles reprinted from the *Journal
of College Student Personnel* and the *Personnel and Guidance Journal.*
Reprinted articles are concerned with the history of student
development, college student characteristics, organizational
dimensions, student services, and preparation programs.

★87   Sanford, Nevitt (ed.). *The American College.* New York:
      Wiley, 1962. 1,084 pages.

This massive landmark volume presents the results of many psychological and social studies of college students. It includes
chapters by many of the leading authorities who had studied
college students at that time. It presents one of the earliest
theories of college student development — that developed by Sanford and his associates. Although it was published more than
twenty-five years ago, some of the chapters in this volume still
are relevant to student services professionals today.

88   Sanford, Nevitt. *Learning After College.* Edited by Craig
      Comstock. Orinda, Calif.: Montaigne, 1980. 280 pages.

In this book outlining the importance of continual growth, Sanford considers communities of scholars and the place of moral
character in personal and organizational life. Sanford begins
with a discussion of personality development and education's
role, then continues with a look at graduate education, academic
culture, and action-research.

College Student Characteristics

★89 Altbach, Philip G., and Kelly, David H. *American Students*. Lexington, Mass.: Heath, 1973. 537 pages.

This volume is divided into two disparate sections. The first is a lengthy chapter discussing student activism and includes a lengthy bibliography dealing with this subject. A second, major portion of the volume consists of over 400 pages of a general bibliography organized according to various topics related to American college students.

★90 Astin, Alexander W. *Four Critical Years: Effects of College on Beliefs, Attitudes, and Knowledge*. San Francisco: Jossey-Bass, 1977. 293 pages.

This book presents the results of Astin's study of a national sample of 220,000 students from 300 institutions, followed up five to ten years after their freshman year in college. Changes that occurred among college students are examined by measuring outcomes regarding attitudes, career plans and aspirations, persistence, achievement, and satisfaction with college.

91 Astin, Alexander W.; Green, Kenneth C.; and Korn, William S. *The American College Freshman: Twenty-Year Trends, 1966–1985*. Los Angeles: Higher Education Institute, University of California, Los Angeles, 1987. 104 pages.

This report summarizes data collected from twenty years of national surveys of entering college freshmen. Trends in academic preparation, demographic data, educational and career plans, attitudes regarding controversial issues, and student values are summarized, both in the text and in a large number of tables.

92   DeCoster, David A., and Mable, Phyllis (eds.). *Understanding Today's Students*. New Directions for Student Services, no. 16. San Francisco: Jossey-Bass, 1981. 125 pages.

The results of a study designed to accurately portray students' motivations, goals, and expectations are discussed. This sourcebook relies heavily on descriptions of college life verbalized by students themselves. Chapters range from personal values to social issues and activism.

★93   Feldman, Kenneth A., and Newcomb, Theodore M. *The Impact of College on Students*. 2 vols. San Francisco: Jossey-Bass, 1969. 644 pages.

These two volumes contain a comprehensive summary and review of 1,500 research reports, both published and unpublished, dealing with the impact of higher education on students. In Volume One the results are summarized and discussed by types of institutions, types of residence, and types of majors. In Volume Two all of the studies are listed, primarily in tabular form, along with the summary of the results, usually stated briefly in short phrases or in statistical form.

94   Horowitz, Helen L. *Campus Life: Undergraduate Cultures from the End of the 18th Century to the Present*. New York: Knopf, 1987. 330 pages.

This book is an interesting history of collegiate life and culture in the United States during the last two centuries and up into the 1980s. The roles that three types of college students—college men and women, outsiders, and rebels—play in the student cultures of various generations are analyzed. The changes that college students have experienced in regard to their daily lives, academic goals, career objectives, and social expectations are chronicled in this comprehensive, historical study of campus life.

★95 Katchadourian, Herant A., and Boli, John, *Careerism and Intellectualism Among College Students: Patterns of Academic and Career Choice in the Undergraduate Years.* San Francisco: Jossey-Bass, 1985. 324 pages.

The authors report the results of a longitudinal study of a random sample of students at Stanford University who were interviewed and administered lengthy questionnaires each year until they graduated. The authors divided the students into four types—careerists, intellectuals, strivers, and the unconnected—and proceeded to discuss how each type meets problems faced in college and makes career decisions.

★96 Lenning, Oscar T.; Munday, Leo A.; Johnson, O. Bernard; Vander Well, Alan R.; and Brue, Eldon J. *The Many Faces of College Success and Their Nonintellective Correlates: The Published Literature Through the Decade of the 60s.* Iowa City, Iowa: American College Testing Program, 1974. 552 pages.

This volume is an exhaustive compilation of studies related to college student development and student success during one decade. A large number of studies are listed, with some of the more pertinent ones briefly described. Includes those dealing with intellectual, social, cultural, moral, motivational, and religious development.

★97 Lenning, Oscar T.; Munday, Leo A.; Johnson, O. Bernard; Vander Well, Alan R.; and Brue, Eldon J. *Nonintellective Correlates of Grades, Persistence, and Academic Learning in College: The Published Literature Through the Decade of the 60s.* Iowa City, Iowa: American College Testing Program, 1974. 272 pages.

This particularly extensive and exhaustive review of research studies deals with factors related to grades, persistence, and learning in higher education. Although covering studies completed during only one decade, it is a valuable resource for anyone planning to conduct research related to this topic.

★98   Levine, Arthur. *When Dreams and Heroes Died: A Portrait of Today's College Student.* San Francisco: Jossey-Bass. 1980. 157 pages.

This report for the Carnegie Council on Policy Studies in Higher Education provides a description of the undergraduate in the late 1970s. Based on surveys of 95,000 students, surveys of administrators at 870 institutions, and campus visits to institutions across the country, this report compares the attitudes and anxieties of students of earlier times with those of the late 1970s. These latter students appear more materialistic, competitive, distrustful, and self-indulgent. Experiences of recent history and aspects of current society are related to these attitude changes. Included are student attitudes toward politics, educational and social interests, their own futures, and the state of campus activism. A summary of student attitudes since colonial times is included to provide a unique perspective in regard to the more current generation of college students.

99   Trent, James W., and Medsker, Leland L. *Beyond High School: A Psycho-Sociological Study of 10,000 High School Graduates.* San Francisco: Jossey-Bass, 1968. 333 pages.

This book contains the results of a longitudinal study examining the personal and vocational development of a large sample of high school graduates. Patterns of college attendance, persistence in college, and a comparison of those who attended college with those who did not were included in this early research effort.

100 Upcraft, M. Lee; Gardner, John N.; and Associates. *The Freshman Year Experience: Helping Students Survive and Succeed in College.* San Francisco: Jossey-Bass, 1989. 480 pages.

This book presents evidence of the importance and impact of the freshman year in college in determining the extent to which students will survive and succeed in subsequent years. Strategies, programs, and services that foster students' educational progress and adjustment during the first year are presented. The benefits of a freshman seminar along with its organization and content are described.

101 Yamamoto, Kaoru (ed.). *The College Student and His Culture: An Analysis.* Boston: Houghton Mifflin, 1968. 493 pages.

This edited volume contains chapters written by a number of authorities in the field who were widely respected at the time this volume was published. The chapters cover a span ranging from the time students consider college while still in high school through students in graduate and professional programs. Certain chapters contain material that continues to be relevant for higher education today.

Special Student Populations

For key resources on special student services, see entry nos. 398–410 in Chapter Eight.

102 Upcraft, M. Lee; Gardner, John N.; and Associates. *The Freshman Year Experience: Helping Students Survive and Succeed in College.* San Francisco: Jossey-Bass, 1989. 480 pages.

For a description of this work see entry no. 100.

Adult Students

103 Bowen, Howard R. *Adult Learning, Higher Education, and the Economics of Unused Capacity.* Princeton, N.J.: College Entrance Examination Board, 1980. 45 pages.

A brief report, based on statistics, indicating a potential increasing enrollment of adult students at the same time as the predicted decrease in traditional-aged students. It includes suggestions for developing effective programs for older students and support services for the unique needs of these adults.

★104 Cross, K. Patricia. *Adults as Learners: Increasing Participa-*
      tion and Facilitating Learning. San Francisco: Jossey-Bass,
      1981. 300 pages.

In this book the author reviews the relevant literature and data
regarding the adult learner and draws conclusions regarding
future trends and developments in lifetime learning. Included
are psychological models of adult learning, the social inequities
that are further increased through continued education, and the
requirement for continuing education by various professional
groups. The author makes the point that we are becoming a
learning society because of increasing societal and technological
change and thus it is becoming increasingly imperative that
adults engage in lifelong learning. The challenges to higher
education administrators and faculty brought by this new clien-
tele are set forth.

105 Heermann, Barry; Enders, Cheryl Coppeck; and Wine,
     Elizabeth (eds.). *Serving Lifelong Learners.* New Directions
     for Community Colleges, no. 29. San Francisco: Jossey-
     Bass, 1980. 107 pages.

This sourcebook comprehensively discusses recruiting adult
learners, designing and implementing programs to meet the
needs of adult learners, and training community college faculty
to more effectively serve this new student population.

106 Kasworm, Carol E. (ed.). *Educational Outreach to Select*
     Adult Populations. New Directions for Continuing Educa-
     tion, no. 20. San Francisco: Jossey-Bass, 1983. 116
     pages.

This sourcebook describes programs and support services designed to extend opportunities to special populations, marketing
programs effectively.

107 Pennington, Floyd D. (ed.). *Assessing Educational Needs of Adults*. New Directions for Continuing Education, no. 7. San Francisco: Jossey-Bass, 1980. 107 pages.

An overview of the theory and practice of analyzing the educational needs of adults, this sourcebook discusses applications for program evaluation and development for marketing.

108 Peterson, David A. *Facilitating Education for Older Learners*. San Francisco: Jossey-Bass, 1983. 342 pages.

This book summarizes the relevant research, societal trends, and implications and educational consequences of an aging society. Programs and courses for the retraining of older workers are considered, as well as preretirement and postretirement educational programs. Problems and preferences of older learners are discussed, and a strong recommendation is made that institutions pay a great deal more attention to the educational needs and desires of the older population.

109 Peterson, Richard E. "Opportunities for Adult Learners." In Arthur W. Chickering and Associates, *The Modern American College: Responding to the New Realities of Diverse Students and a Changing Society*. San Francisco: Jossey-Bass, 1981, pp. 306–327.

Different types of resources for adult education are enumerated and discussed in this chapter. In addition to secondary and post-secondary educational institutions, the author includes informal resources such as travel or electronic media, and non-school organizations such as industrial training programs and the military services. The role of post-secondary institutions in providing educational opportunities for adults and necessary changes in institutional policies toward adult learning are addressed. For a description of Chickering's complete work see entry no. 85.

110 Schlossberg, Nancy K.; Lynch, Ann Q.; and Chickering, Arthur W. *Improving Higher Education Environments for Adults: Responsive Programs and Services from Entry to Departure.* San Francisco: Jossey-Bass, 1989. 304 pages.

In this book the authors present a range of policies, programs, and services that can be provided to meet the needs of adult students. A number of real-life vignettes are provided to illustrate the differences between the needs of adult learners and those of traditional undergraduates. Chapters deal with the understanding of adult learners and programs designed to attract adult learners to higher education and to support their progress from entry to graduation.

111 Shriberg, Arthur (ed.). *Providing Student Services for the Adult Learner.* New Directions for Student Services, no. 11. San Francisco: Jossey-Bass, 1980. 97 pages.

This edited monograph consists of nine chapters by different authors who are concerned with understanding adult learners and designing programs to meet their needs. An overview of adult development theory is provided and the challenges and implications for the student services profession of this growing population are addressed. Proposals for recruiting adults and adapting traditional student services to meet their needs are provided.

112 Solmon, Lewis C., and Gordon, Joanne J. *The Characteristics and Needs of Adults in Post-Secondary Education.* Lexington, Mass.: Heath, 1981. 157 pages.

This book summarizes information regarding the demographics, finances, college plans, and life goals of full-time adult (over twenty-one) entering freshmen from national surveys of entering freshmen conducted by the Cooperative Institutional Research Program. Trends in the characteristics of these adult freshmen are examined over the thirteen-year period covered by the surveys analyzed in this study.

113 Steltenpohl, Elizabeth, and Shipton, Jane. "Facilitating a Successful Transition to College for Adults." *Journal of Higher Education,* 1986, *57*(6), 637–658.

For a description of this work see entry no. 257.

114 Tough, Alan. "Interests of Adult Learners." In Arthur W. Chickering and Associates, *The Modern American College: Responding to the New Realities of Diverse Students and a Changing Society.* San Francisco: Jossey-Bass, 1981, pp. 296–305.

This chapter examines the concept of lifelong learning and the needs of adult learners, and discusses the implications of these concepts and needs for institutions of higher education. For a description of Chickering's complete work see entry no. 85.

Minority Students

For key resources on the recruitment of minorities, see entries 226–230 in Chapter Five.

★115 Astin, Alexander, W. *Minorities in American Higher Education: Recent Trends, Current Prospects, and Recommendations.* San Francisco: Jossey-Bass, 1982. 263 pages.

This publication of the Higher Education Research Institute presents and analyzes longitudinal studies of the educational progress and status of blacks, Chicanos, Puerto Ricans, and American Indians at undergraduate and graduate levels, with recommendations for changes needed to increase educational access for these minorities.

116 Elam, Julia C. (ed.). *Blacks on White Campuses: Proceedings of a Special NAFEO Seminar.* Lanham, Md.: University Press of America, 1983. 99 pages.

This edited volume is a collection of essays developed from a seminar sponsored by the National Association for Equal Opportunity in Higher Education. The essays deal with issues that impact both black students and black staff on white campuses. Several chapters deal with the role and status of black administrators at white institutions. A model affirmative action program is presented.

117 Fleming, Jacqueline. "Special Needs of Blacks and Other Minorities." In Arthur W. Chickering and Associates, *The Modern American College: Responding to the New Realities of Diverse Students and a Changing Society.* San Francisco: Jossey-Bass, 1981, pp. 279–295.

This chapter discusses developmental issues and the social adjustment of minority students in college, and examines differential influences on black students in predominantly black institutions and predominantly white institutions. For a description of Chickering's complete work see entry no. 85.

★118 Fleming, Jacqueline. *Blacks in College: A Comparative Study of Students' Success in Black and in White Institutions.* San Francisco: Jossey-Bass, 1984. 276 pages.

The findings of a major study on black college students are presented, indicating that white colleges may be less supportive of black students' development than are black colleges. Recommendations for improving the educational opportunities and development of all students at both black and white colleges are included for administrators, counselors, and other student service professionals.

119 Green, Bert F. (ed.). *Issues in Testing: Coaching, Disclosure, and Ethnic Bias.* New Directions for Testing and Measurement, no. 11. San Francisco: Jossey-Bass, 1981. 127 pages.

For a description of this work see entry no. 243.

120 Hsia, Jayjia. *Asian-Americans in Higher Education and at Work*. Hillsdale, N.J.: Erlbaum, 1988. 238 pages.

This book summarizes the backgrounds, abilities, aspirations, and achievements of Asian American students in colleges and universities. The high proportion of Asian Americans entering higher education and the problems associated with their concentration in certain colleges and in certain majors are pointed out in the data presented by this author.

121 Lang, Marvel, and Ford, Clintia A. (eds.). *Black Student Retention in Higher Education*. Springfield, Ill.: Thomas, 1988. 111 pages.

For a description of this work see entry No. 265.

122 Nettles, Michael T. *Toward Black Undergraduate Student Equality in American Higher Education*. Westport, Conn.: Greenwood Press, 1988. 217 pages.

This edited volume consists of ten chapters that analyze black undergraduate students' backgrounds, performances, attitudes, and experiences at various types of colleges and universities. Data regarding black students' performance and experiences on the campus are presented, along with a discussion of the roles that institutions, states, and the federal government play in achieving equality for black students in higher education.

123 Olivas, Michael A. *The Dilemma of Access: Minorities in Two-Year Colleges*. Washington, D.C.: Howard University Press, 1979. 259 pages.

This volume contains a great deal of data concerning minorities in community colleges, including student characteristics, faculty and administrators, academic programs, and support services. Recommendations for action by community colleges are made, based on the data presented in this volume.

124 Pedersen, Paul. *A Handbook for Developing Multicultural Awareness.* Alexandria, Va.: American Association for Counseling and Development, 1988. 216 pages.

This practical guide addresses the improvement of awareness and communication between culturally diverse individuals. Multicultural developmental stages, simulation exercises, and other specific techniques are featured, as well as a discussion of multicultural identity and an emphasis on overcoming cultural stereotypes.

125 Peterson, Marvin W.; Blackburn, Robert T.; Gamson, Zelda F.; Arce, Carlos H.; Davenport, Roselle W.; and Mingle, James R. *Black Students on White Campuses: The Impacts of Increased Black Enrollments.* Ann Arbor: Institute for Social Research of the University of Michigan, 1978. 388 pages.

This book describes a study of the impact, both positive and negative, of black students on thirteen colleges and universities and the responses of the institutions to these students. It includes the perceptions and responses of students, faculty, and administrators and describes the strategies used to address this population.

126 Pruitt, Anne S. (ed.). *In Pursuit of Equality in Higher Education.* Dix Hills, N.Y.: General Hall, 1987. 226 pages.

This edited volume summarizes the findings of a number of research studies undertaken to assess the progress being made toward eliminating inequality of blacks in higher education. Included are studies that examine access to postsecondary education, experiences on black and white campuses, retention, choice of major and career aspiration, and access to graduate and professional education.

127 Thomas, Gail E. (ed.). *Black Students in Higher Education.* Westport, Conn.: Greenwood Press, 1981. 407 pages.

This edited volume contains chapters dealing with a wide variety of issues and problems related to black students in postsecondary education. Access, admissions, academic experiences, career aspirations, and retention are examples of the topics presented.

128 Wright, Doris J. (ed.). *Responding to the Needs of Today's Minority Students.* New Directions for Student Services, no. 38. San Francisco: Jossey-Bass, 1987. 117 pages.

This sourcebook focuses on implementation and development of a range of student services programs for minority students at predominantly white institutions. It discusses the impact of the circumstances of the 1960s on current minority programs and explains how to update these programs to meet changing needs.

Women Students

129 Bernard, Jessie. "Women's Educational Needs." In Arthur W. Chickering and Associates, *The Modern American College: Responding to the New Realities of Diverse Students and a Changing Society.* San Francisco: Jossey-Bass, 1981, pp. 256–278.

This chapter investigates women's educational needs at various developmental stages in their life cycles. These stages are conceptualized as contingency schedules and the author examines the implications of these schedules from a feminist perspective. For a description of Chickering's complete work see entry no. 85.

130 Eaton, Judith S. (ed.). *Women in Community Colleges.* New Directions for Community Colleges, no. 34. San Francisco: Jossey-Bass, 1981. 95 pages.

This discussion of the contributions and opportunities for women in community colleges focuses on the diversity of roles available to women, the special problems of minority women, and the future of women's studies programs.

131 Evans, Nancy J. (ed.). *Facilitating the Development of Women.* New Directions for Student Services, no. 29. San Francisco: Jossey-Bass, 1985. 116 pages.

This sourcebook focuses on the complex needs of women students and ways student services professionals can effectively respond so as to foster women's intellectual, personal, and career growth.

132 Josselson, Ruthellen. *Finding Herself: Pathways to Identity Development in Women.* San Francisco: Jossey-Bass, 1987. 225 pages.

This book reports the results of an interview study of women college seniors in the early 1970s who were then followed up twelve years later. The study examines the effect of childhood experiences, crises, influences, and relationships upon the development of identity status in women.

133 Komarovsky, Mirra. *Women in College: Shaping New Feminine Identities.* New York: Basic Books, 1985. 355 pages.

This book summarizes the results of a survey and interview study of over 200 college women contacted during their freshman, sophomore, and senior years. Their academic, social, and intellectual development is chronicled, with particular attention paid to their orientations regarding careers, marriage, and sex roles.

Other Populations

134 May, Ronald J., and Scher, Murray (eds.). *Changing Roles for Men on Campus.* New Directions for Student Services, no. 42. San Francisco: Jossey-Bass, 1988. 105 pages.

This review of how men's roles have changed in our society and how this affects campus services, particularly programs that serve men, includes a presentation of a developmental profile for men and a discussion of their interaction patterns with their environment.

135 Stewart, Sylvia S. (ed.). *Commuter Students: Enhancing Their Educational Experiences.* New Directions for Student Services, no. 24. San Francisco: Jossey-Bass, 1983. 85 pages.

This edited monograph addresses the characteristics and special needs of commuter students. The diversity of this population is examined, and proposals for changes in student services designed to enhance the development of these students are provided. Additionally, the results of a nineteen-campus study of campus services that are attempting to meet the needs of these students are summarized.

136 Walsh, Patricia A. (Ed.). *Serving New Populations.* New Directions for Community Services, No. 27. San Francisco: Jossey-Bass, 1979, 114 pages.

This edited monograph addresses community college programs targeted at older adults, handicapped students, and women. It describes programs for women returning to the job market, emeritus colleges for older adults, and support services for the handicapped. Methods of evaluating the extent to which services meet the needs of such special populations are described, and successes and failures of innovative programs for these students are analyzed.

Periodicals and Annuals

137 *The American Freshman: National Norms for Fall 19--.* Published annually by the Cooperative Institutional Research Program of the Higher Education Research Institute, University of California, Los Angeles, Calif. 90024.

This annual publication reports the results of a national freshman survey of student characteristics.

138 *College Student Journal.* Published four times a year, additional monographs also published occasionally, P.O. Box 8508, Spring Hill Station, Mobile, Ala. 36608.

This journal addresses college student values, attitudes, opinions, and learning. It also includes issues regarding graduate and professional schools and college preparation.

∽ 4 ∾

Administrative Roles,
Concerns, and Practices

Although many professionals in the student services field are full-time administrators, there are not a large number of important publications dealing specifically with student services administration. Within the total field of general administration, there are many publications that deal with the multiple aspects of administration and administrative processes.

General administration has been studied by psychologists, sociologists, economists, and many others. As a result, there are many books dealing with administration and management of business and industrial enterprises, governmental organizations, and educational organizations. These deal with a variety of topics including personnel administration, public relations, planning, budgeting, and other particular areas and functions carried out by managers and administrators. Although these sources provide much useful information for those in administration and higher education, there are very few resources available that take the knowledge derived in many of these other fields and apply it specifically to student services. Because the topic of administration, and even that of higher education administration, includes a very large bibliography, no attempt has been made here to list more than a few general resources either within or outside of higher education. Those resources that deal specifically with the administration of student services on college and university campuses represent the majority of resources included in this chapter.

Training programs for student services professionals are typically found in one of two departments — counselor education or educational administration. When located in a department of counselor education, the program may or may not be a separate program specifically training student services professionals. The same is true when the program is found in the department of educational administration or more specifically higher education administration. Those programs found in counseling departments tend to provide considerable training in counseling, group dynamics, and other aspects of applied psychology and include a little administration, while those found in departments of educational administration provide considerable training in administration and perhaps a little in counseling.

The field of student affairs generally needs personnel with some training in each area since many entry-level positions involve more counseling and applied psychology and the general philosophy of the field has its basis in psychology and counseling. On the other hand, the career ladder in student services is such that if persons are to advance, they quickly become involved in more administrative work. While an academic faculty member on the campus can move from instructor to full professor without becoming involved in administration, in other parts of the university upward mobility involves taking on greater administrative responsibilities for the management and supervision of larger and larger groups of people and agencies. Thus the application of effective administrative principles and practices becomes increasingly important as one progresses up the student services career ladder. One of the concerns in the student services field is that those graduating from preparation programs have obtained the skills for entry-level positions but lack the knowledge and administrative skills for the middle- and upper-level administrative positions to which they aspire. Accompanying this concern is the question of whether such skills should be a part of the initial training programs or introduced through some program of continuing education or further training.

The literature reviewed in this chapter attempts to cover

a number of aspects of student services administration and includes a few sources outside the student services field that were felt to be particularly relevant for student affairs professionals. It should be pointed out that in addition to the resources listed in this chapter, a number of chapters from the edited books dealing with the entire profession also address administrative topics. These resources are referenced in Chapter Two and include chapters in the volumes edited by Delworth and Hanson (1989, no. 23); Eddy, Dameron, and Borland (1980, no. 24); Harrington (1974, no. 25); and Owens, Witten, and Bailey (1982, no. 26). A number of specific aspects of administration — such as management systems, staff development, planning, and budgeting — are found in these chapters as they relate specifically to the administration of student services agencies.

The first group of resources deals specifically with the administration of student services and is followed by resources dealing with administrative roles in student affairs, and administrative methods and techniques in student affairs administration. Legal considerations have become an increasingly important and aggravating aspect of student services administration. The result has been a number of publications dealing with legal issues confronting various student services; these are referenced in the next section. The third section contains references related to particular concerns of student affairs administrators, followed by resources dealing with evaluations and accountability that also represent knowledge and methods necessary for administrators on most campuses. Certain resources in more general higher education administration that include topics of particular interest to student affairs professionals are presented in the fourth section. Lastly, several recent volumes dealing with general administrative theory and practice were selected from the large number available and are included to illustrate other important sources of information for this specialty area. Earlier important resources by such authorities as Peter Blau, Peter Drucker, Amitai Etzioni, and Talcott Parsons are not included, but a reader may find references to their works summarized in more recent volumes that are included.

Administration of Student Services

139 Ambler, David A. "Designing and Managing Programs: The Administrator Role." In Ursula Delworth, Gary R. Hanson, and Associates, *Student Services: A Handbook for the Profession.* (2nd ed.) San Francisco: Jossey-Bass, 1989, pp. 247–264.

In this chapter the author discusses an administrative model of student services. He points out the conflict between the roles of administrator and educator. He enumerates the functions of an administrative program and the elements that make up such a program. For a description of Delworth and Hanson's complete work see entry no. 23.

140 Appleton, James R.; Briggs, Channing M.; and Rhatigan, James J. *Pieces of Eight: Rites, Roles, and Styles of the Dean of Eight Who Have Been There.* Portland, Oreg.: NASPA Institute of Research and Development, 1978. 194 pages.

This compendium of professional information was obtained by interviewing eight long-experienced student affairs administrators. Chapters deal with the functions of student affairs, the roles of deans and vice-presidents, with considerable advice for new professionals.

141 Barr, Margaret J.; Keating, Lou A.; and Associates. *Developing Effective Student Services Programs: Systematic Approaches for Practitioners.* San Francisco: Jossey-Bass, 1985. 353 pages.

This book contains fourteen chapters by leaders in the student affairs field dealing with the planning and implementing of quality student programs. An extensive annotated bibliography of related writings is included.

142 Deegan, William A. *Managing Student Affairs Programs: Methods, Models, Muddles.* Palm Springs, Calif.: ETC Publications, 1981. 223 pages.

This book provides a guideline for attempting to apply modern management concepts to student affairs. It includes four comprehensive case studies of institutions that have used this approach.

143 Foxley, Cecelia H. (ed.). *Applying Management Techniques.* New Directions for Student Services, no. 9. San Francisco: Jossey-Bass, 1980. 100 pages.

This volume is one of the few that borrows principles and techniques from the field of business administration and applies them to student affairs. Included are discussions of organizational development, systems analysis, management by objectives, and management information systems.

144 Kuh, George D. (ed.). *Understanding Student Affairs Organizations.* New Directions for Student Services, no. 23. San Francisco: Jossey-Bass, 1983. 113 pages.

Kuh presents an insightful discussion of the assumptions about student affairs organizations and alternatives to the bureaucratic model, including an examination of several major theories of organizations.

145 Miller, Theodore K.; Winston, Roger B., Jr.; and Mendenhall, William R. (eds.). *Administration and Leadership in Student Affairs.* Muncie, Ind.: Accelerated Development, 1983. 350 pages.

This volume contains chapters by twenty-three educators dealing with administrative theory and practice, organizational development, ethical practices, legal guidelines, programming, resource and facilities management, and professional growth and practices. The general focus of the chapters is the encouragement of student development through administrative procedures and strategies, along with strategies to obtain and manage the resources needed to fulfill this mission.

146 Owens, Hilda F.; Witten, Charles H.; and Bailey, Walter R. (ed.). *College Student Personnel Administration: An Anthology.* Springfield, Ill.: Thomas, 1982. 391 pages.

For a description of this work see entry no. 26.

147 Upcraft, M. Lee, and Barr, Margaret J. *Managing Student Affairs Effectively.* New Directions for Student Services, no. 41. San Francisco: Jossey-Bass, 1988. 94 pages.

A guide to the daily management of student affairs, this volume shares the expertise of seasoned professionals. Included are strategies for improving functioning in many areas.

Administrative Roles in Student Affairs

148 Banning, James H. "Creating a Climate for Successful Student Development: The Campus Ecology Manager Role." In Ursula Delworth, Gary Hanson, and Associates, *Student Services: A Handbook for the Profession.* (2nd ed.) San Francisco: Jossey-Bass, 1989, pp. 304–322.

This chapter describes an ecological approach that focuses on the interaction between the individual and the environment. Applications of this approach to college campuses are discussed and illustrated. For a description of Delworth and Hanson's complete work see entry no. 23.

149 Brodzinski, Frederick R. "The Changing Role of the Chief Student Personnel Administrator." *Journal of College Student Personnel,* 1980, *21,* 3–8.

This article reports the results of a study on the current functional responsibilities of chief student personnel officers in a random sample of over 400 two- and four-year institutions. Responsibility for the different functions was compared with results of a similar study conducted fifteen years earlier.

150 Cohen, Robert D. (ed.) *Working with Parents of College Students.* New Directions for Student Services, no. 32. San Francisco: Jossey-Bass, 1985. 110 pages.

This monograph deals with the topic of how institutional administrators can establish and maintain unofficial relationships with parents of students. Included are such subjects as the Buckley Amendment, parent orientation, information regarding student financial aid for parents, and the organization of a parents' organization.

151 Delworth, Ursula (ed.). *Training Competent Staff.* New Directions for Student Services, no. 2. San Francisco: Jossey-Bass, 1978. 99 pages.

This volume addresses another important role of the student services professional: training staff members. The concepts covered range from interpersonal skills, training innovations, and manuals to supervision and teaching others to be trainers.

152 Eddy, John; Dameron, Joseph D.; and Borland, David T. (eds.). *College Student Personnel Development, Administration, and Counseling.* (2nd ed) Lanham, Md.: University Press of America, 1980. 538 pages.

For a description of this work see entry no. 24.

153 Hamilton, M. Kathryn, and Meade, Charles J. (eds.). *Consulting on Campus.* New Directions for Student Services, no. 5. San Francisco: Jossey-Bass, 1979. 104 pages.

This sourcebook provides assistance to student affairs professionals in consulting with administrators and faculty to influence policy. It provides an outline of training and evaluation procedures and an examination of models of consultation.

154 Kuh, George D., and McAlleenan, Andrea C. *Private Dreams, Shared Visions: Student Affairs Work in Small Colleges.* Columbus, Ohio: National Association of Student Personnel Administrators, 1986. 119 pages.

This edited monograph concentrates on student affairs work in small colleges. The eight chapters deal with the role of student affairs work in the planning, programming, and learning that takes place in smaller institutions. The majority of the eighteen contributors to this book hold leadership roles in student affairs in small colleges.

155 Kuh, George D.; Whitt, Elizabeth J.; and Schedd, Jill D. *Student Affairs 2001: A Paradigmatic Odyssey.* Alexandria, Va.: American Association for Counseling and Development, 1987. 137 pages.

For a description of this work see entry no. 51.

156 McCarthy, Jane E. (ed.). *Resolving Conflict in Higher Education.* New Directions for Higher Education, no. 32. San Francisco: Jossey-Bass, 1980. 96 pages.

This volume outlines the use of neutral mediators in settling disputes within institutions, whether between administrators and faculty or handling student grievances.

157 Tilley, David C.; Benezet, Louis T.; Katz, Joseph; and Santeau, William. *The Student Affairs Dean and the President: Trends in Higher Education.* Ann Arbor, Mich.: ERIC Counseling and Personnel Services Clearinghouse, 1979. 90 pages.

This publication examines trends in higher education and the role of the student affairs dean in addressing these trends. Considerable focus is on the relationships and collaboration with other administrators and the academic faculty.

Administrative Methods and Techniques

158 Brodzinski, Frederick R. (ed.). *Utilizing Futures Research.* New Directions for Student Services, no. 6. San Francisco: Jossey-Bass, 1979. 104 pages.

This sourcebook describes how projecting and preparing for future developments can increase the overall effectiveness of student services by improving goal setting and decision making, and the subsequent planning and delivery of student services.

159 Brown, Robert D. *Performance Appraisal as a Tool for Staff Development.* New Directions for Student Services, no. 43. San Francisco: Jossey-Bass, 1988. 116 pages.

This practical guide for student affairs professionals demonstrates the utilization of performance appraisal as a tool for staff development. Included are specific advice and recommendations for conducting the appraisal process.

160 Dalton, John C. "Enhancing Staff Knowledge and Skills." In Ursula Delworth, Gary Hanson, and Associates, *Student Services: A Handbook for the Profession.* (2nd ed.) San Francisco: Jossey-Bass, 1989; pp. 533–551.

In this chapter the author presents the purposes of a staff development program and suggests curriculum topics for an organized staff development program within an institution. He also suggests other opportunities for development including academic classes, job rotation, job enrichment, and mentoring. For a description of Delworth and Hanson's complete work see entry no. 23.

161 Deegan, W. L.; Steele, B. H.; and Thielen, T. B. *Translating Theory into Practice: Implications of Japanese Management Theory for Student Personnel Administrators.* Columbus, Ohio: National Association of Student Personnel Administrators, 1985. 84 pages.

This volume outlines some of the management concepts and techniques developed in Japanese organizations and discusses how they can be applied by American student personnel administrators — in the same way that American business and industrial organizations have found some of them to be useful. Included are several models that are recommended for experimentation in student affairs, such as job rotations and quality circles.

162   Eddy, John P.; Inchassi, Roy S.; and Associates. *Higher Education Student Affairs Leadership: Programming, Budgeting, and Evaluating.* Minneapolis: Burgess, 1986. 252 pages.

This volume includes thirty-five chapters dealing with such topics as leadership, administration, communication, and evaluation.

163   Ender, Steven C., and Winston, Roger B. (eds.). *Students as Paraprofessional Staff.* New Directions for Student Services, no. 27. San Francisco: Jossey-Bass, 1984. 111 pages.

This overview of effective ways to employ students as part-time staff in a variety of student services programs is a complete guide to planning, recruiting, training, supervising, compensating, and evaluating student assistants.

164   Kalsbeek, David H. "Managing Data and Information Resources." In Ursula Delworth, Gary Hanson, and Associates, *Student Services: A Handbook for the Profession.* (2nd ed.) San Francisco: Jossey-Bass, 1989, pp. 493–512.

This chapter describes systems which make use of data processing information to provide data for management support and for decision making in student services. The complexity in establishing and making use of such information systems is discussed as well as the advantages that they can provide. For a description of Delworth and Hanson's complete work see entry no. 23.

165 Schuh, John H., and Rickard, Scott T. "Planning and Budgeting." In Ursula Delworth, Gary Hanson, and Associates, *Student Services: A Handbook for the Profession.* (2nd ed.) San Francisco: Jossey-Bass, 1989, pp. 461–492.

This chapter presents various approaches to planning with particular emphasis on strategic planning. The authors describe several approaches to budgeting including line-item, program, and zero-base budgeting. The chapter concludes with advice for those preparing budgets for particular student affairs units. For a description of Delworth and Hanson's complete work see entry no. 23.

166 Sheehan, Bernard S. (ed.). *Information Technology: Innovations and Applications.* New Directions for Institutional Research, no. 35. San Francisco: Jossey-Bass, 1982. 121 pages.

This sourcebook discusses the advances in computer and communication technologies and ways of applying these advances to college and university operations. Numerous applications are illustrated, including data base systems, personal computers, digital networks, and videodiscs.

Legal Considerations

167 American Association of Collegiate Registrars and Admissions Officers. *Legal Guide for Admissions and Registrars.* Washington, D.C.: American Association of Collegiate Registrars and Admissions Officers, 1986. 80 pages.

For a description of this work see entry no. 239.

168 Barr, Margaret J. (ed.). *Student Affairs and the Law.* New Directions for Student Services, no. 22. San Francisco: Jossey-Bass, 1983. 105 pages.

As higher education reflects society at large and increasingly uses the courts to settle differences, legal challenges to the student services profession become more apparent. This issue attempts to provide basic knowledge regarding legal processes and implications for the student services administrator without a strong background in law.

169 Barr, Margaret J. "Legal Issues Confronting Student Affairs Practice." In Ursula Delworth, Gary Hanson, and Associates, *Student Services: A Handbook for the Profession.* (2nd ed.) San Francisco: Jossey-Bass, 1989, pp. 80–111.

This chapter presents the legal statutes and decisions likely to have implications for student services professionals, including constitutional rights of students, civil rights laws, contract law, and tort liability. The author emphasizes the importance to student services of having some understanding of the law. A list of legal citations of relevant court cases is included. For a description of Delworth and Hanson's complete work see entry no. 23.

170 Barr, Margaret J., and Associates. *Student Services and the Law: A Handbook for Practitioners.* San Francisco: Jossey-Bass, 1988. 430 pages.

This book contains chapters by a number of authors covering the laws and legal decisions that affect the various student services areas. Topics include students' constitutional rights, contractual agreements, civil rights, and institutional liability. They are covered in more depth than in the work described in entry no. 168.

171 Gibbs, Annette. "Mandatory Student Activity Fees: Educational and Legal Considerations." *Journal of College Student Personnel,* 1980, *21,* 535–540.

For a description of this work see entry no. 521.

172 Hammond, Edward H., and Shaffer, Robert H. *The Legal Foundations of Student Personnel Services in Higher Education.* Alexandria, Va.: American College Personnel Association, 1978. 174 pages.

One of the first to cover legal issues specific to student services, this volume discusses freedom of speech and organization rights, the right to privacy, due process requirements, and staff liability.

173 Owens, Hilda F. (ed.). *Risk Management and the Student Affairs Professional.* Columbus, Ohio: National Association of Student Personnel Administrators, 1984. 146 pages.

This monograph discusses the risks involved in student affairs work on the campus, the responsibilities that accompany these risks, and steps that may be taken to minimize them. Included are chapters dealing with the legalities of the relationships between students, student affairs organizations, and the institutions. Also discussed are the particular risks involved in campus activities and those of a residential campus.

174 Pavela, Gary. *The Dismissal of Students with Mental Disorders: Legal Issues, Policy Considerations, and Alternative Responses.* Asheville, N.C.: College Administration Publications, 1985. 97 pages.

This publication covers the laws, court decisions, hearings, and due process requirements dealing with the dismissal of students suffering from mental disorders. Specific standards and procedures are recommended, along with the need for proper referral and follow-up.

Legal Periodicals

175 *Journal of College and University Law.* A quarterly journal
   published by the National Association of College and
   University Attorneys, Suite 650, One Dupont Circle
   NW, Washington, D.C. 20036.

This journal publishes articles, commentaries on recent cases,
and legislation dealing with legal issues and developments relevant to higher education.

176 Young, D. Parker, and Gehring, Donald D. *The College
   Student and the Courts: Cases and Commentary.* Published
   quarterly by College Administration Publications,
   Department PC, P.O. Box 8492, Asheville, N.C. 28814.

Court cases that have resulted in significant decisions related
to higher education are summarized in this newsletter. Summaries include the facts and issues in the case, the court's decision, the reasoning of the court, and comments by the editors.
Cumulative index sections are published periodically.

Special Concerns for Student Affairs Administrators

177 Bordner, Diane C., and Peterson, David M. *Campus
   Policing: The Nature of University Police Work.* Lanham,
   Md.: University Press of America, 1983. 260 pages.

This study examines the conflicts arising in regard to provisions
of protective services on campus that typically involve law en-
forcement, as well as the more traditional security functions of
plant protection, preventative maintenance, and the tension between these functions and the regulation of student conduct.

★178 Kotler, Phillip, and Fox, Karen F. A. *Strategic Marketing
   for Educational Institutions.* Englewood Cliffs, N.J.: Prentice-Hall, 1985. 396 pages.

The purpose of this book is to provide a practical model of
marketing strategies adopted from sales and marketing organi-

zations and applied to institutions of higher education. It includes examples of how marketing techniques such as market segmentation and positioning strategies have been employed by various colleges and universities throughout the country. Chapters also deal with the application of these techniques to student retention and fund raising. This aspect makes the book of interest to such college and university administrators as presidents, deans, alumni and development officers, and admissions personnel.

179 Zinner, Ellen S. (ed.). *Coping with Death on Campus.* New Directions for Student Services, no. 31. San Francisco: Jossey-Bass, 1985. 113 pages.

This sourcebook identifies the issues of student loss and student death, and the unique position that student affairs professionals can establish in addressing these issues. A general discussion of student loss and grief is presented, followed by chapters that deal specifically with actions to be taken when a student dies.

Evaluation of Student Services

180 Braskamp, Larry A., and Brown, Robert D. (eds.). *Utilization of Evaluative Information.* New Directions for Program Evaluation, no. 5. San Francisco: Jossey-Bass, 1980. 101 pages.

This comprehensive look at effective utilization of evaluative information considers ways to ensure that evaluation findings are used in policy formation and administrative decision making.

181 Council for the Advancement of Standards. *CAS Self-Assessment Guides.* College Park: University of Maryland Office of Student Affairs, 1989.

Eighteen separate self-assessment guides designed to assist student affairs professionals in conducting evaluations of programs and services are provided for each of eighteen student services areas. They are designed to assess program effectiveness, or for strategic planning, self-study, or accreditation purposes. Each guide includes the general standards and guidelines previously developed for that functional area by CAS. (See Miller, Thomas, and Looncy, no. 183.)

182 Kuh, George D. (ed.). *Evaluation in Student Affairs.* Alexandria, Va.: American College Personnel Association, 1979. 180 pages.

Chapters by various authors present issues and strategies for evaluating student services, paying particular attention to a half dozen common student services agencies. Three case studies are also presented.

183 Miller, T. K.; Thomas, W. L.; and Looncy, S. (eds.). *Council for the Advancement of Standards: Standards and Guidelines for Student Services/Developmental Programs.* Council for the Advancement of Standards for Student Services/ Development, 2108 North Administration Building, University of Maryland, College Park, Md. 20742. 1986. 111 pages.

This publication outlines standards and guidelines for the professional practice of student affairs programs in higher education. In addition to the general standards it includes sixteen sections covering the various functional areas within student services, such as career planning and placement, residential life programs, judicial programs, student activities, and so on. The publication is intended to assist institutions in improving their student services operations.

184 Scott, Robert A. *Determining the Effectiveness of Campus Services.* New Directions for Institutional Research, no. 41. San Francisco: Jossey-Bass, 1984. 93 pages.

This sourcebook is a guide for assessing the quality and efficiency of student services, public relations, library services, computing services, self-study activities, and alliances with business and industry. Included is a discussion of possible impediments to evaluation processes, as well as indicators of effective functioning in each area.

Higher Education Administration

185 Astin, Alexander W., and Scherrei, Rita A. *Maximizing Leadership Effectiveness: Impact of Administrative Style on Faculty and Students.* San Francisco: Jossey-Bass, 1980. 238 pages.

This book reports results of a study of leadership styles in over forty private colleges. Four types of leadership styles are described and also summarized are the strengths and weaknesses of each, and the types of institutions in which each is likely to be found. The authors argue for a student-oriented administrative style in order to increase student involvement in the academic and collegiate experience. They maintain that the greater the physical and emotional energy students expend in that experience, the greater will be their learning and development.

186 Blake, Robert, R.; Mouton, Jane Srygley; and Williams, Martha Shipe. *The Academic Administrator Grid: A Guide to Developing Effective Management Teams.* San Francisco: Jossey-Bass, 1981. 423 pages.

Blake and Mouton's management grid from business and industry is applied to college and university administration. This widely used conceptual framework grid identifies five primary styles of leadership and describes how they differ. Case examples illustrating various leaders are included.

187 Brown, David G. (ed.). *Leadership Roles of Chief Academic Officers.* New Directions for Higher Education, no. 47, San Francisco: Jossey-Bass, 1984. 104 pages.

This edition of New Directions for Higher Education features an assessment of qualities needed by academic officers and the functions identified as necessary by college presidents, provosts, and other chief academic officers. Management strategies and suggestions for anticipating the future are also included.

188 Dressel, Paul L. *Administrative Leadership: Effective and Responsive Decision Making in Higher Education.* San Francisco: Jossey-Bass, 1981. 243 pages.

With an emphasis on decision making, this guide for administrative leadership examines current problems and explores strategies for making decisions and identifying the values that should underlie these deliberations. Emphasis is also placed on crisis management and ongoing evaluation as a preventative strategy.

189 Eble, Kenneth E. *The Art of Administration: A Guide for Academic Administrators.* San Francisco: Jossey-Bass, 1978. 174 pages.

With a viewpoint that academic administration is public service, Eble addresses what personal characteristics are required and how they can be acquired or strengthened. He also discusses how to execute managerial tasks and exercise authority diplomatically to provide effective academic leadership.

190 Falender, Andrew J., and Merson, John C. (eds.). *Management Techniques for Small and Specialized Institutions.* New Directions for Higher Education, no. 42. San Francisco: Jossey-Bass, 1983. 100 pages.

This sourcebook presents an overview of techniques for administrators of small and specialized institutions to enhance their effectiveness as managers. A discussion of strategies includes topics such as financial planning and development, information systems, staff organization, and admissions.

191 Hoverland, Hal; McInturff, Pat; Rohm, C. E. Tapie, Jr., (eds.). *Crisis Management in Higher Education.* New Directions for Higher Education, no. 55. San Francisco: Jossey-Bass, 1986. 120 pages.

This compendium of effective strategies for coping with crisis in a variety of higher education settings outlines ways of determining problems, developing solutions, and implementing policies that will help to avert future crises. The methods for this volume were drawn from administrators at all levels and from different types of institutions.

192 Mortimer, Kenneth P., and McConnell, T. R. *Sharing Authority Effectively: Participation, Interaction, and Discretion.* San Francisco: Jossey-Bass, 1978. 322 pages.

In view of changes made in academic authority during the 1960s and 1970s, this volume examines how current patterns of centralization are having an impact on campus authority. Includes a discussion of accountability and policy dilemmas brought about by the changes in authority.

193 Vaughan, George B., and Associates. *Issues for Community College Leaders in a New Era.* San Francisco: Jossey-Bass, 1983. 275 pages.

This volume presents twelve chapters examining issues and problems faced by community colleges. Issues discussed that are related to student services include community college students, transfer problems, access for disadvantaged students, career issues for women students, remedial education, and model student services programs.

194 Walker, Donald E. *The Effective Administrator: A Practical Approach to Problem Solving, Decision Making, and Campus Leadership.* San Francisco: Jossey-Bass, 1979. 226 pages.

This book outlines a theoretical perspective and specific principles and procedures for effective educational administration. The nature of colleges and universities is considered, as well as ways to include faculty, students, and others in the decision-making process.

195 Warren, Jonathan R. (ed.). *Meeting the New Demand for Standards.* New Directions for Higher Education, no. 43. San Francisco: Jossey-Bass, 1983. 101 pages.

This examination of ways administrators can promote and evaluate standards of ensuring quality of learning provides information regarding ways of communicating these standards to various constituencies.

196 Wilson, James A. (ed.). *Management Science Applications to Academic Administration.* New Directions for Higher Education, no. 35. San Francisco: Jossey-Bass, 1981. 128 pages.

Drawing on management techniques and theories from administrative science and organizational analysis, this volume applies these concepts to improve the organization of colleges and universities.

Ethics in Higher Education Administration

197 Baca, M. Carlota, and Stein, Ronald H. (eds.). *Ethical Principles, Practices, and Problems in Higher Education.* Springfield, Ill.: Thomas, 1983. 290 pages.

This book presents a discussion of ethics in a variety of situations, including moral discourse, ethical responsibility of faculty, teaching of ethics, due process, ethics and amateur athletics, ethics and computing facilities, and ethics in collective bargaining.

198 Franklin, Phyllis; Moglen, Helene; Zatlin-Boring, Phyllis; and Angres, Ruth. *Sexual and Gender Harassment in the Academy: A Guide for Faculty, Students, and Administrators.* New York: Modern Language Association of America, 1981. 75 pages.

This guide presents a brief overview of the types of harassment problems and the policies and practices to address them on the college campus. It discusses various types of harassing behaviors and includes advice on how to deal with them. Institutional policies and procedures designed to increase the understanding of the nature of sexual harassment and ways to respond to complaints are presented.

199 Gehring, Donald; Nuss, Elizabeth M.; and Pavela, Gary. *Issues and Perspectives on Academic Integrity.* Columbus, Ohio: National Association of Student Personnel Administrators, 1986. 25 pages.

This brief monograph presents the data relating to the extent of student academic dishonesty, moral issues, legal issues and due process procedures, and the roles of various members of the campus community in responding to this problem. The final section of the monograph includes a set of recommendations for developing a program to improve the academic integrity of a campus.

200 Stein, Ronald H., and Baca, M. Carlota (eds.). *Professional Ethics in University Administration.* New Directions for Higher Education, no. 33. San Francisco: Jossey-Bass, 1981. 100 pages.

With a focus on self-regulation, this volume addresses the major ethical issues confronting academic administrators in the 1980s. Issues discussed include marketing abuses, sexual harassment, discrimination, and low academic standards.

General Administration Theory and Practice

201 Hersey, Paul, and Blanchard, Kenneth H. *Management of Organizational Behavior: Utilizing Human Resources.* (4th ed.) Englewood Cliffs, N.J.: Prentice-Hall, 1982. 343 pages.

This volume is a general introduction to managerial theory and organizational behavior. Theories of management and leader behavior are briefly presented, environmental variables and expectations described, and methods of determining and increasing managerial effectiveness are discussed.

202 Hoy, Wayne K., and Miskel, Cecil G. *Educational Administration: Theory, Research, and Practice.* (3rd ed.) New York: Random House, 1987. 488 pages.

Although designed primarily as a text in public school administration, this book also contains a summary of theory and research in a number of areas including bureaucracies, informal organizations, leadership styles, communication, and decision making.

203 Kimbrough, Ralph B., and Nunnery, Michael Y. *Educational Administration: An Introduction.* (2nd ed.) New York: Macmillan, 1983. 588 pages.

This book contains an overview of educational administration and administrative theory. Although aimed primarily at administrators in public education, portions of the book deal more generally with administrative theory, administrative functions, and administrative decision making.

204 Scott, W. Richard. *Organizations: Rational, Natural, and Open Systems.* Englewood Cliffs, N.J.: Prentice-Hall, 1981. 381 pages.

In this volume the various theories and models of management and organizations are discussed and critiqued. They are conceptualized as falling into the three general types of systems and the rationale for each is presented by the author.

⚜ 5 ⚜

Recruitment, Admissions, and Retention

On a number of campuses, an administrator is given the responsibility for overall enrollment management, which includes all three functions of recruitment, admission, and retention. Because these functions share common goals, and occasionally common administrators, they will be considered together in this chapter.

Recruitment involves attracting students, including persuading their counselors, parents, and peers to show an interest in the institution. Hopefully, as a result of interest generated by recruitment activities, students will apply for admission to the institution. Admission procedures encompass the selection, entry, and subsequent matriculation of the student at the institution. Lastly, retention services are concerned with helping students persist at the institution and include overall attempts to reduce attrition rates.

As the literature indicates, professionals performing these three functions have become more sophisticated in fulfilling their responsibilities to the institution regarding both the marketing procedures used for recruitment and the various types of orientation, counseling, and advising programs designed to retain students. Since student satisfaction is particularly important in combatting attrition, efforts are increasingly made to increase the "match" that students feel with the institution and to provide other activities that help the student adjust and successfully matriculate.

The extensive literature dealing with the field of college admissions has been produced over a long period of time. A heightened interest in the subjects of recruitment and retention, however, is considerably more recent in origin. As long as an institution had more students applying for admission than it could handle, there was less concern with either the recruitment of additional applicants or with retaining those students who were dropping out for one reason or another, since there were plenty of replacements who could be admitted the following year. With the decrease in the number of traditional college-age students along with the increased difficulty many students are experiencing financing the costs of college, success in the recruitment, admission, and retention of students has become increasingly important for many institutions. Indeed, many higher education institutions have become dependent upon these services for their very survival, and for a few the recruitment of an adequate entering class has become a crucial and desperate effort.

Admissions officers have learned much from the business sector regarding marketing strategies and techniques to assist in the recruitment process. Highly sophisticated marketing strategies have included using high-tech methods to identify target populations likely to yield the greatest number of applicants and have emphasized the importance of repeated contacts, both personal and through mailings. Admission staffs at many institutions have doubled and tripled in size, and the budgets allocated to their work have greatly increased. The status of the director of the admissions office on the campus has risen substantially along with the administrative level at which he/she operates. This increased salary and status have often been accompanied by increased pressure to "produce or else." Questions have been raised regarding the ethics of some of the recruitment and admissions efforts that have been undertaken by certain institutions.

In this chapter, references related to the general demographics of potential student populations are included, followed by references concerned with enrollment management systems and marketing strategies. The recruitment of minorities has received increasing emphasis and requires concentrated efforts on the part of admissions personnel. These references are found in the next section, while other related topics concerning minority students such as financial aid and student characteristics are referenced in other chapters (Chapter Six and Chapter Three).

The following two sections of this chapter deal with admissions policies and the administration of admissions offices. The use of scholastic aptitude tests in the admissions process has always been a controversial subject, and some of the publications of those who support and those who oppose the use of these tests are contained in the testing literature in the next section. In spite of such controversy, the use of test results both for admissions decisions and for the purposes of educational advising has not significantly diminished over the past several decades.

The next sections include sources related to college admissions counseling and school-college articulation. These are followed by references related to orientation programs since it is important for students' adjustment to higher education that they receive adequate orientation to campus life. A strong orientation program is seen as the first step in combatting student attrition. While orientation on many campuses has as its primary concern the processing of incoming students in regard to their registration and housing, programs are now also concerned with the additional functions of assisting with their social and academic adjustment. The field is becoming increasingly professionalized, with full-time orientation directors rather than several student services and academic staff having part-time responsibilities. It is also becoming more comprehensive — beginning before the student arrives on the campus and continuing during the first term or throughout the first year. Regularly scheduled courses, either elective or required, that deal with topics related to orientation to higher education which were once popular and then almost extinct, are now beginning to emerge again on various campuses. The literature related to orientation is continuing to grow, addressing both the traditional students as well as transfer students, adult students, and others who make up the increasing diversity of students in higher education.

Having spent considerable time and money obtaining numbers of applicants to the institution, the problem then is to turn the applicants into students who actually matriculate. If, after having begun as freshmen, large numbers of them drop out, then much of the money and effort expended to attract them in the first place is at least partially wasted. Therefore the need to reduce student attrition and to retain as many students as possible until graduation has become important.

Student retention at many institutions has become a total campus effort involving staff and student services, the business offices, the residence halls, and faculty in the academic departments. That students feel involved with the campus, that they receive adequate counseling and advising, and that they feel they have received individual attention are all seen as important aspects of student retention. Staff members throughout the campus are expected to be alert to students who might consider leaving and are expected to do what they can to assist the student to choose to remain. This increased emphasis has resulted in a number of recent books and monographs written to assist institutions in combatting student attrition.

Available to the professionals in the admissions field are several journals that make important contributions to the literature in this area. For many years *College and University,* a journal published by the American Association of Collegiate Registrars and Admissions Officers, has contained numerous articles of interest to those in the admissions field. The journal published by the National Association of College Admissions Counselors is also an important resource. The two major national college admissions testing institutions — the College Entrance Examination Board and the American College Testing Program — publish numerous monographs containing research and other types of articles for those in the admissions field. The College Entrance Examination Board publishes the *College Board Review,* another useful periodical dealing with collegiate admissions.

Since admissions policies and information are of interest to many in higher education, the periodical literature related to admissions is also found occasionally in a wide variety of journals dealing with higher education. At one time the *Personnel and Guidance Journal* (now *Journal of Counseling and Development*) published a number of articles related to higher education admissions, but changes in the editorial policies of that journal over the years have substantially eliminated it as a source of admissions literature. Although the generalist journals in student services such as the *Journal of College Student Development* and the *NASPA Journal* contain literature from across the student services areas, they are not often a source of literature on admissions.

The literature in the field of student orientation presents a very different picture. Without the existence of a major journal dealing with student orientation, the periodical source for this literature is found primarily in the generalist journals. By far the largest source of articles in the field of orientation is the *Journal of College Student Development.* The *NASPA Journal* is the second most frequent source, and the *Journal of the National Association for Women Deans, Administrators, and Counselors* ranks third for journal articles dealing with orientation.

Since financial aid has become an important facet of the recruitment and admissions processes, admissions counselors must now become familiar with several aspects of student financial aid. These periodicals, and especially the *College Board Review,* often include articles dealing with financial aid that are useful to those in admissions. Since both the College Entrance Examination Board and the American College Testing Program also collect information from students and parents regarding their financial situations and provide information upon which to base student financial aid, the activities and the publications of both of these organizations reflect these overlapping functions.

As these two organizations totally dominate the admissions testing programs at the undergraduate level, they also produce a number of publications dealing with the use of scholastic aptitude tests in the recruitment, admissions, and advising process.

This chapter lists those resources in the areas of admissions and retention that are important for student affairs professionals who deal with these topics. Another type of literature dealing with college admissions not referenced in this volume consists of the many college guides published to assist students in their college choice decisions. Certain of these provide objective information about colleges: *The College Handbook,* published by the College Board; *Peterson's Guide to the Four-Year Colleges, The Competitive Colleges,* and *The Regional College Guides,* all published by Peterson's Guides; and *The College Planning Search Book,* published by the American College Testing Program. Another type of college guide is more subjective in nature and includes various descriptive paragraphs designed to differentiate among the institutions and give a "flavor" of their campuses. These include *The Insider's Guide to the Colleges,* published by the Yale Daily News; *The Best Buys in College Education,* published by the New York Times; *The Black Student's Guide to College,* published by E. P. Dutton; and *The Public Ivys,* published by Viking Penguin Books.

Admissions Demographics

★205 American Council on Education. *Fact Book on Higher Education, 1989*–90. Riverside, N.J.: Macmillan, 1989. 304 pages.

This book of statistics and graphs begins with demographic data on the entire U.S. population, often broken down by state and region, and then moves to enrollment data in all levels of higher education and in different types of institutions. Data are typically broken down by sex, race, graduate, and undergraduate students. This is a useful source for anyone in higher education needing to examine enrollments and enrollment trends among different types of students at different levels and in different types of institutions.

206 Baldridge, J. Victor; Kemerer, Frank R.; and Green, Kenneth C. *The Enrollment Crisis: Factors, Actors, and Impacts.* Washington, D.C.: American Association for Higher Education, 1982. 69 pages.

In this monograph the results of a national survey of college presidents and admissions officers are reported and combined with demographic trends to yield radically different expected futures for different types of institutions. Recruitment strategies and student retention programs are discussed as ways some institutions can attempt to offset some of these pessimistic projections.

★207 Birnbaum, Robert. *Maintaining Diversity in Higher Education.* San Francisco: Jossey-Bass, 1983. 209 pages.

This book examines diversity in American higher education, particularly emphasizing trends that took place over the two decades between 1960 and 1980. An ecological model of diversity is presented that particularly emphasizes the impact of environment upon the populations of students. Recommendations for encouraging diversity and for coping with diverse populations are also included.

★208 Breland, Hunter M.; Wilder, Gito; and Robertson, Nancy J. *Demographics, Standards, and Equity: Challenges in College Admissions.* Published by and available from each of the sponsoring associations/agencies, 1986.

This publication is a report of a survey of undergraduate admissions policies, practices, and procedures sponsored by the American Association of Collegiate Registrars and Admissions Officers, the American College Testing Program, the College Board, the Educational Testing Service, and the National Association of College Admissions Counselors.

209 Zemsky, Robert, and Odell, Penny. *The Structure of College Choice.* New York: College Examination Board, 1983. 113 pages.

In this volume the authors provide an examination of geographic, demographic, and economic influences on college enrollments and the possible results that these will have on future patterns of college enrollment.

Enrollment Management

210 Hossler, Don. *Enrollment Management, an Integrated Approach.* New York: College Entrance Examination Board, 1984. 168 pages.

This short book reviews the literature from a wide variety of fields dealing with enrollment management. Some of the subjects include marketing strategies, financial aid, pricing, the achievement of a good student-institutional fit, the impact of college, the outcomes of college, and factors related to college choice.

211 Hossler, Don. *Creating Effective Enrollment Management Systems.* New York: College Entrance Examination Board, 1986. 141 pages.

This book presents concepts, issues, and models of enrollment management, along with case studies at four different institutions.

212 Hossler, Don (ed.). *Managing College Enrollments.* New Directions for Higher Education, no. 53. San Francisco: Jossey-Bass, 1986. 112 pages.

This edited book provides chapters that discuss the various aspects that make up an effective program of enrollment management. It includes such areas as marketing strategies, student services, academic advising, orientation, career counseling and placement, and the problem of retention. It is designed to give an overall introduction to the topic and gives an overview of the many aspects of a total enrollment management model.

★213 Kemerer, Frank R.; Baldridge, J. Victor; and Green, Kenneth C. *Strategies for Effective Enrollment Management.* Washington, D.C.: American Association of State Colleges and Universities, 1982. 198 pages.

In this book the authors discuss the various aspects that make up an effective program of enrollment management. They include strategies for marketing, organizing admissions offices, and addressing the problem of retention. The emphasis is upon the overall planning, organization, and decision-making processes and responsibilities for effective enrollment management aimed at assisting institutions to survive the enrollment decline of the 1980s. Strategic planning in marketing programs and admissions policies and programs to combat student attrition are described.

214 Muston, Ray. *Marketing and Enrollment Management in State Universities.* Iowa City, Iowa: American College Testing Program, 1985. 162 pages.

This is a report of a study of enrollment management practices and the results of those practices at over fifty state universities on which various types of ACT data were available. A method for evaluating enrollment performance is presented along with much data in chart and tabular form.

Marketing Higher Education

215 Barton, David W., Jr. (ed.). *Marketing Higher Education.* New Directions for Higher Education, no. 21. San Francisco: Jossey-Bass, 1978. 91 pages.

This volume deals with strategies and issues of concern to many institutions with smaller numbers of traditionally aged students. Chapters include those dealing with identifying a desirable student pool, effective "courting" of students, strategies of financial aid packaging, and the administration of admissions programs.

216 Beder, Hal (ed.). *Marketing Continuing Education.* New Directions for Continuing Education, no. 31. San Francisco: Jossey-Bass, 1986. 110 pages.

A comprehensive volume detailing the development of successful marketing programs for continuing education programs, this book focuses on ways to improve recruitment and retention, how to analyze resources and needs, and how to increase participant satisfaction. It offers practical information regarding the use of promotional media, determining program costs, and choice of program locations is also provided.

217 Colloquium on Marketing, Student Admissions, and Public Interest. *Marketing in College Admissions: A Broadening of Perspectives.* New York: College Entrance Examination Board, 1980. 170 pages.

This volume contains papers by ten authors dealing with a variety of issues in the field of college marketing and admissions.

★218 Ihlanfeldt, William. *Achieving Optimal Enrollments and Tuition Revenues: A Guide to Modern Methods of Market Research, Student Recruitment, and Institutional Pricing.* San Francisco: Jossey-Bass, 1980. 267 pages.

This book discusses strategies that can assist an institution in obtaining a larger and stronger applicant pool in a highly competitive applicant market. It contains an overview of the types of information needed to be collected and how to plan and implement marketing efforts based on this information. A number of practical examples of the collection and interpretation of this information are included in the final section of the book.

219 Keim, William A., and Keim, Marybelle C. (eds.). *Marketing the Program.* New Directions for Community Colleges, no. 36. San Francisco: Jossey-Bass, 1981. 127 pages.

This sourcebook is a comprehensive overview of the development and implementation of a marketing program for community colleges. The views of college presidents, faculty members, information directors, and marketing specialists are included.

★**220** Kotler, Phillip, and Fox, Karen F. A. *Strategic Marketing for Educational Institutions.* Englewood Cliffs, N.J.: Prentice-Hall, 1985. 396 pages.

This book provides a practical model of marketing strategies from sales and marketing organizations adapted to institutions of higher education. It includes examples of how such marketing techniques as market segmentation and positioning strategies have been employed by various colleges and universities throughout the country. Chapters also deal with the application of these techniques to student retention and to fund raising. This makes the book of interest to other college and university administrators, including presidents, deans, and alumni and development officers, as well as admissions personnel.

221 Lay, Robert S., and Endo, Jean J. (eds.). *Designing and Using Marketing Research.* New Dimensions for Institutional Research, no. 54. San Francisco: Jossey-Bass, 1987. 120 pages.

This monograph contains nine chapters dealing with the use of marketing research in higher education. Subjects discussed include studying institutional images, assessing the market for students, assessing the market for new programs, identifying market segments, and developing and implementing marketing programs.

222 Litten, Larry H. (ed.). *Issues in Pricing Undergraduate Education.* New Directions for Institutional Research, no. 42. San Francisco: Jossey-Bass, 1984. 103 pages.

This sourcebook examines the variety of pricing strategies being used by institutions to balance the increasing costs of providing a quality education while attempting to reduce the burden of the impact of pricing policies on consumers. Justifiable pricing practices are considered.

223 Litten, Larry H.; Sullivan, Daniel; and Brodigan, David E. *Applying Market Research in College Admissions.* New York: College Entrance Examination Board, 1983. 303 pages.

This volume contains a case study of the marketing research program conducted by Carleton College over a ten-year period. A description of the research conducted on the campus as well as that carried out in six large metropolitan areas is included, along with examples of the questionnaires used and a brochure that resulted from these surveys.

★224 Riesman, David. *On Higher Education: The Academic Enterprise in an Era of Rising Student Consumerism.* San Francisco: Jossey-Bass, 1981. 421 pages.

This volume considers the impact on higher education of the student as a consumer. Institutional marketing strategies are discussed, along with the rise of students as consumers and the consequent decline of the dominance of the faculty. Methods by which students can bring about constructive change through this influence are outlined, particularly in regard to institutions providing accurate information to guide students in their choice among the various institutions. Warnings are voiced, and certain actions and changes are recommended for higher education as the student applicant becomes a courted customer.

225 Smith, Virginia C., and Hunt, Susan (eds.). *The New Guide to Student Recruitment and Marketing.* Washington, D.C.: Council for the Advancement and Support of Education, 1986. 95 pages.

This book is subtitled "The Best of Case Currents" and is a collection of articles from the monthly magazine *Currents.* The large number of articles deal with advertising, recruitment tools, publications, using alumni, and marketing research. A number of the articles provide rather specific applied information for practitioners to use in their marketing efforts.

Recruitment of Minorities

★226 Adolphus, Stephen H. (ed.). *Equality Postponed: Continuing Barriers to Higher Education in the 1980s.* New York: College Entrance Examination Board, 1984. 156 pages.

The report of a 1982 conference dealing with programs for disadvantaged students in higher education, this book examines trends in access to higher education among various minorities. Types of programs that have been developed and new issues and problems that have arisen are also presented and analyzed.

227 Carter, Glenda F. *Financial Aid and Black Students.* Lanham, Md.: University Press of America, 1988. 62 pages.

For a description of this work see entry no. 293.

228 Cheatham, Harold E. "Recruiting Minority Students: An Evaluation." *Journal of College Student Personnel,* 1982, *23,* 29–32.

This publication contains the results of a survey of 1,800 black students whose verbal and numeric scores on the College Board totalled at least 1,000. This population was found to be highly recruited and offered numerous attractive options.

★229 Duran, Richard P. *Hispanics' Education and Background: Predictors of College Achievement.* New York: College Board Publications, 1983. 150 pages.

The author presents an extensive review of the literature of studies related to Hispanic entry into, and success in, American institutions of higher education. Statistics related to the completion of high school and entry into college and graduate schools are analyzed, along with those dealing with the achievement of Hispanic students, both in high school and in various types of colleges and universities. Studies of the validity of high school grades, test scores, and other factors related to the prediction of Hispanics' college grades are reviewed, and suggestions are made regarding their use.

230 Green, Madeleine E. (ed.). *Minorities on Campus: A Handbook for Enhancing Diversity.* Washington, D.C.: American Council on Education, 1989. 199 pages.

Chapters in this book deal with strategies for recruiting and retaining larger numbers of minority undergraduate, graduate, and professional students. The importance of an institution-wide approach and specific steps to increase minority participation are presented. Included are profiles of three institutions that have made significant progress in developing an institution-wide commitment to diversity.

Admissions Policy

231 American Council on Education. *College Admissions Policies Toward GED Applicants.* Washington, D.C.: American Council on Education, 1982. 63 pages.

This book contains the results of a survey concerning the admissions policies for applicants who received a high school equivalency certificate based on scores on the General Educational Development test. Admissions policies regarding GED applicants (95 percent of the institutions admit GED applicants), along with the minimum scores and other information required, are summarized.

232 Goetz, M. E., and Johnson, L. *State Policies for Admission to Higher Education.* New York: College Entrance Examination Board, 1985. 31 pages.

This monograph reports the results of a survey of admissions practices for public higher education institutions in the fifty states. Minimum statewide admissions standards in regard to high school records, scores on admissions tests, and required patterns of high school course work are described, along with the extent to which individual institutions were permitted to impose additional requirements. Recent changes in policies and anticipated future changes are also reported.

233 Kitgaard, Robert. *Choosing Elites*. New York: Basic Books, 1985. 267 pages.

The processes of making decisions about admission to undergraduate and professional schools in high-status universities are examined. Included is a discussion of the problems of predicting which will be the most successful (variously defined) from groups of highly qualified applicants.

234 Kuh, George D. "Admissions." In William T. Packwood (ed.), *College Student Personnel Services*. Springfield, Ill.: Thomas, 1977, pp. 3–50.

This chapter reviews the research literature on college admissions through 1975. Topics include admissions programs, administration, policies, and prediction. An extensive list of references is included. For a description of Packwood's complete work see entry no. 27.

235 McCormack, Wayne (ed.). *The Bakke Decision: Implications for Higher Education Admissions*. Washington, D.C.: American Council on Education, 1978. 61 pages.

This report is an analysis of the Bakke decision and the several opinions of the different justices of the Supreme Court. The report analyzes the various objectives to be served by race and ethnic group–conscious admissions programs and presents several models of admissions procedures and criteria that can be used to serve these objectives.

★236 Sacks, Herbert S., and Associates. *Hurdles: The Admissions Dilemma in American Higher Education*. New York: Atheneum, 1978. 364 pages.

This book contains a group of essays by a number of authorities dealing with aspects of admission to colleges and professional schools. The essays describe the impact of admissions experiences upon applicants, admissions directors, and institutions.

237 Willingham, W. W., and Breland, H. M. *Personal Qualities and College Admissions.* New York: College Entrance Examination Board, 1982. 258 pages.

This book offers the results of an extensive study in which admissions information, test scores, a follow-up questionnaire, academic performance, and persistence information were gathered on 500 students admitted to each of nine private liberal arts colleges. Included in the extensive data regarding the relationship of various characteristics to academic performance and persistence is the conclusion that personal qualities added only very slightly to the accuracy of predicting freshman grades based on high school rank and scholastic aptitude test scores alone.

Admissions Administration

★238 American Association of Collegiate Registrars and Admissions Officers and National Association of College Admissions Officers and National Association of College Admissions Counselors. *Professional Development Guidelines for Admissions Officers — A Self Audit.* Washington, D.C.: American Association of Collegiate Registrars and Admissions Officers, 1984. 168 pages.

This monograph is designed to assist admissions professionals in evaluating and improving their admissions programs. It consists of statements of principles concerning various functions of admissions services and a checklist to evaluate the extent to which each principle is being successfully achieved. A list of significant readings accompanies each principle and checklist.

★239 American Association of Collegiate Registrars and Admissions Officers. *Legal Guide for Admissions and Registrars.* Washington, D.C.: American Association of Collegiate Registrars and Admissions Officers, 1986. 80 pages.

This monograph provides a legal guide for admissions issues and procedures, student financial aid, academic and dismissal procedures, and the confidentiality and regulations regarding student records.

★240 Quann, C. James, and Associates. *Admissions, Academic Records, and Registrar Services: A Handbook of Policies and Procedures.* San Francisco: Jossey-Bass, 1979. 481 pages.

This handbook on admissions and records policies and procedures is sponsored by the American Association of Collegiate Registrars and Admissions Officers (AACRAO). It includes chapters dealing with such topics as admissions organization and policies, planning the academic calendar and schedule, administering registration and record keeping procedures, producing institutional research and conducting a commencement. Examples of procedures for both two-year and four-year, public and private institutions are included.

Admissions Testing

★241 Anderson, Scarvia B., and Coburn, Louisa V. (eds.). *Academic Testing and the Consumer.* New Directions for Testing and Measurement, no. 16. San Francisco: Jossey-Bass, 1982. 156 pages.

A consideration of long-standing testing principles and practices, this volume presents the opinions of testing experts, college officials, counselors, students, and parents. The assumptions regarding the purposes, benefits, and uses of tests are also explored.

242 Daves, Charles W. (ed.). *The Uses and Misuses of Tests: Examining Current Issues in Educational and Psychological Testing.* San Francisco: Jossey-Bass, 1984. 133 pages.

This volume contains a collection of contributions from specialists who addressed the 1983 conference of the Educational Testing Service on the uses and misuses of tests. Issues include public concerns, professional standards for test use, the value of standardized testing as an indicator of learning, the effect of test results on the admission of minorities, and legal constraints on test usage.

★243 Green, Bert F. (ed.). *Issues in Testing: Coaching, Disclosure, and Ethnic Bias.* New Directions for Testing and Measurement, no. 11. San Francisco: Jossey-Bass, 1981. 127 pages.

This volume provides an analysis of three important issues in the use of testing. The discussion includes such questions as how much admissions test scores improve with coaching, how test item disclosure affects test equating, and whether current tests are biased against minorities.

244 Messick, Samuel. *The Effectiveness of Coaching for the SAT: Review and Reanalysis of Research from the 50s to the FTC.* Princeton, N.Y.: Educational Testing Service, 1980. 135 pages.

This report presents a critique of the Federal Trade Commission's study of coaching for the Scholastic Aptitude Test (SAT). It includes a complex reanalysis of earlier studies and presents evidence regarding the relatively negligible increase in scores that is typically achieved through a coaching program.

245 Preer, Jean L. *Competence, Admissions, and Articulation: Returning to the Basics in Higher Education.* Washington, D.C.: Association for the Study of Higher Education, 1983. 105 pages.

In this monograph competence testing is described and compared with standardized testing for use in college admission. Recommendations include less reliance on test scores and more consideration of other factors.

246 Schrader, William B. (ed.). *Admissions Testing and the Public Interest.* New Directions for Testing and Measurement, no. 9. San Francisco: Jossey-Bass, 1981. 114 pages.

This publication of conference papers from the 1980 Educational Testing Service Conference focuses on a variety of important testing issues. It includes a discussion of equity in admissions testing, test preparation and interpretation, and the effects of governmental regulations.

Admissions Counseling

247 Commission on Pre-College Guidance and Counseling. *Keeping the Options Open — Recommendations.* New York: College Entrance Examination Board, 1986. 43 pages.

This report presents recommendations concerning precollege guidance and counseling in the schools, especially for students with "limited access to postsecondary education." The report emphasizes the role that counselors play in precollege counseling and proposes a broader role involving parents and younger adolescents, with particular attention to helping disadvantaged students enter and remain in college.

★248 Lowery, William R., and Associates. *College Admissions Counseling: A Handbook for the Profession.* San Francisco: Jossey-Bass, 1982. 618 pages.

This edited volume contains thirty-two chapters by different authors dealing with many aspects involving the recruitment, selection, and advising of students related to college admission. Subjects covered include recruitment and selection strategies and procedures, admissions testing, financial aid, special services, enrollment management, recruitment and selection of minorities, adult, and transfer students. The book is aimed at both school counselors and college admissions personnel.

★249 Manski, Charles F., and Wise, David A. *College Choice in America.* Cambridge, Mass.: Harvard University Press, 1983. 221 pages.

This volume describes a major research study on college choice based on results from the National Longitudinal Survey of the High School Class of 1972. Included are numerous factors related to students' choices and college attendance patterns, such as college test scores, parental education and income, availability

of scholarships and grants, college costs and institutional decisions. Models and prediction equations are presented relating
to application, admission, financial aid, academic achievement,
and attrition.

School-College Articulation

250 Daly, William (ed.). *College-School Collaboration: Apprais-
ing the Major Approaches.* New Directions for Teaching and
Learning, no. 24. San Francisco: Jossey-Bass, 1985. 129
pages.

A practical guide for administrators, this volume provides a
critical examination of the efforts to strengthen relationships between institutions of higher education and secondary schools.
A description and evaluation of ten model programs is included,
along with recommendations for program development, taking
into consideration regional needs, program content, and gaining local support.

Orientation

251 Cohen, Robert D. (Ed.). *Working with Parents of College
Students.* New Directions for Student Services, no. 32.
San Francisco: Jossey-Bass, 1985. 110 pages.

For a description of this work see no. 150.

252 Cohen, Robert D., and Jody, Ruth. *Freshman Seminar:
A New Orientation.* Boulder, Colo.: Westview Press, 1978.
144 pages.

In this book the authors present a practical guide for establishing
a freshman orientation course based on their experiences in
developing one at Hunter College. A rationale is presented for
such a course, and the components are described, along with
the purposes of each. Student affairs personnel provide instruction in the course, along with regular academic faculty.

253 Dannells, Michael, and Kuh, George D. "Orientation." In William T. Packwood (ed.), *College Student Personnel Services.* Springfield, Ill.: Thomas, 1977, pp. 102–124.

This chapter reviews research literature related to college orientation programs, including types of programs, administration and funding, and general purposes and objectives. Also included are programs designed to meet the needs of special student groups. For a description of Packwood's complete work see entry no. 27.

254 Kramer, Gary L., and Washburn, Rob. "The Perceived Orientation Need of New Students." *Journal of College Student Personnel,* 1983, *24,* 311–319.

This article summarizes the results of a survey of student-perceived needs conducted both before and after an extensive orientation program at a large private university. Academic and career planning needs were ranked highest, and personal and social needs lowest in both surveys.

255 Levitz, Randi, and Noel, Lee. "Connecting Students to Institutions: Keys to Retention and Success." In M. Lee Upcraft, John N. Gardner, and Associates, *The Freshman Year Experience: Helping Students Survive and Succeed in College.* San Francisco: Jossey-Bass, 1989, pp. 65–81.

In this chapter the authors discuss the problem of attrition and the various factors related to students dropping out. They present types of programs and efforts that institutions can make to help students remain and be successful in college. Emphasis is placed on helping students become involved with the institution and with higher education. For a description of Upcraft and Gardner's complete work see entry no. 100.

256 Perigo, Donald J., and Upcraft, M. Lee. "Orientation
      Program." In M. Lee Upcraft, John N. Gardner, and
      Associates, *The Freshman Year Experience: Helping Students
      Survive and Succeed in College.* San Francisco: Jossey-Bass,
      1989, pp. 82–94.

In this chapter the authors present an overview of orientation
programming. Orientation programs are discussed in terms of
a three-phased effort—pre-admissions, pre-enrollment, and initial enrollment prior to the start of classes. Examples are given
of activities from a number of campuses to illustrate each of the
types of orientation activities. The authors emphasize the importance of basing orientation activities on principles of student
development. For a description of Upcraft and Gardner's complete work see entry no. 100.

257 Steltenpohl, Elizabeth, and Shipton, Jane. "Facilitating
      a Successful Transition to College for Adults." *Journal
      of Higher Education,* 1986, *57*(6), 637–658.

This article describes a course that had been offered over a six-
year period for adults entering or reentering college, designed
to provide an introductory learning experience and an understanding of higher education. The results of a study of the needs,
aspirations, and outcomes of students participating in the course
along with several case studies are also presented.

★258 Upcraft, M. Lee (ed.). *Orienting Students to College.* New
      Directions for Student Services, no. 25. San Francisco:
      Jossey-Bass, 1984. 116 pages.

Orientation as a means to ease student transition to college and,
consequently, to enhance retention is the focus of this volume.
The goals and methodologies of an effective orientation program
are presented, as well as a discussion of orienting minority,
disabled, returning adult, and transfer students.

259 Upcraft, M. Lee; Gardner, John N.; and Associates. *The Freshman Year Experience: Helping Students Survive and Succeed in College.* San Francisco: Jossey-Bass, 1989. 480 pages.

For a description of this work see entry no. 100.

Transfer Student Articulation

260 Kintzer, Frederick C. (ed.). *Improving Articulation and Transfer Relationships.* New Directions for Community Colleges, no. 39. San Francisco: Jossey-Bass, 1982. 115 pages.

This volume addresses methods for facilitating the transfer of students from high schools to two-year colleges, and from the two-year colleges to four-year institutions. Practical solutions for many problems encountered in the transfer process are presented. The volume concludes with an investigation of the reasons students transfer, including why students may "reverse" transfer from universities to community colleges.

261 Kintzer, F. C., and Wattenbarger, J. L. *The Articulation/Transfer Phenomenon: Patterns and Directions.* Washington, D.C.: American Association of Community and Junior Colleges, 1985. 76 pages.

This report summarizes current statistics about students transferring between community colleges and four-year institutions in California and other states, and the patterns of transfer that exist. Patterns of transfer are also reported for several foreign countries. Issues and concerns about articulation between these institutions in the future are considered.

Student Retention

★262 Astin, Alexander, W. *Preventing Students from Dropping Out.* San Francisco: Jossey-Bass, 1975. 204 pages.

The results of a longitudinal study of college dropouts provides information regarding student and institutional characteristics that may indicate potential dropouts. Student services policies such as financial aid and residential arrangements that may reduce the dropout rate are discussed.

263 Astin, Alexander, W. *Four Critical Years: Effects of College on Beliefs, Attitudes, and Knowledge.* San Francisco: Jossey-Bass, 1977. 293 pages.

For a description of this work see entry no. 90.

264 Cowart, Susan C. *What Works in Student Retention in State Colleges and Universities.* Iowa City, Iowa: American College Testing Program, 1987. 145 pages.

This monograph reports the results of a survey conducted by the American Association of State Colleges and Universities (AASCU) of the attrition and retention studies and programs in almost 200 of the member institutions. In the first half of the book the attrition studies are summarized and the results of various retention programs are described and evaluated. The second half of the monograph consists of copies of retention activity report forms that describe the various retention programs that have been undertaken on the responding campuses.

265 Lang, Marvel, and Ford, Clintia A. (eds.). *Black Student Retention in Higher Education.* Springfield, Ill.: Thomas, 1988. 111 pages.

This edited volume is designed to provide a resource for the recruitment, retention, and eventual graduation of black college students. Chapters describe approaches that have obtained some degree of success at particular institutions.

266 Noel, Lee (ed.). *Reducing the Dropout Rate.* New Directions for Student Services, no. 3. San Francisco: Jossey-Bass, 1978. 122 pages.

This analysis of why students drop out of college includes a discussion of successful retention programs and solutions for addressing the attrition problems of nontraditional populations.

★267 Noel, Lee; Levitz, Randy; Saluri, Diana; and Associates. *Increasing Student Retention: Effective Programs and Practices for Reducing the Dropout Rate.* San Francisco: Jossey-Bass, 1985. 484 pages.

This book contains chapters by a number of authors presenting different programs and techniques for reducing student attrition rates. Five different groups of students most likely to drop out are suggested as targets for various programs. The roles played by various student affairs agencies in reducing attrition and the importance of developing campus-wide support for retention programs is emphasized. A number of case studies representing successful programs are presented.

268 Pascarella, Ernest T. (ed.). *Studying Student Attrition.* New Directions in Institutional Research, no. 36. San Francisco: Jossey-Bass, 1982. 104 pages.

This sourcebook explores methods of studying student attrition, including causes, number of dropouts, and alternatives for reducing attrition.

269 Terrell, Melvin C., and Wright, Doris J. (eds.). *From Survival to Success: Promoting Minority Student Retention.* Washington, D.C.: National Association of Student Personnel Administrators, 1989. 133 pages.

This volume is designed as a guide for developing and evaluating programs designed to retain ethnic minority students. Social and psychological factors that affect minority student success are examined.

★270 Tinto, Vincent. *Leaving College: Rethinking the Causes and Cures of Student Attrition.* Chicago: University of Chicago Press, 1987. 246 pages.

In this volume the author has attempted to combine some early sociological theories with information from contemporary attrition studies to provide a model for approaching the problem of student retention. The book includes a comprehensive survey of the literature dealing with student attrition. The model emphasizes the decisions that students make on an individual basis to drop out of college and outlines actions institutions can take to deal with student attrition.

Periodicals

★271 *Journal of College Admissions* (formerly NACAC Journal). Published quarterly by the National Association of College Admissions Counselors, King Street Station, 1800 Diagonal Road, Suite 430, Alexandria, Va. 22314.

This journal includes articles of interest to those in the admissions field dealing with marketing, college admission, and student financial aid. Subscription included with National Association of College Admissions Counselors membership.

272 *College and University.* Published quarterly by the American Association of Collegiate Registrars and Admissions Officers (AACRAO), One Dupont Circle, Washington, D.C. 20036.

This journal contains issue-oriented, theoretical, and research-based articles dealing with the various functions of college and university registrars and admissions staff.

★273 *College Board Review.* Published quarterly by the College Entrance Examination Board, 45 Columbus Avenue, New York, N.Y. 10023.

This journal contains articles primarily aimed at those in the field of college and university admissions. It includes articles dealing with the financing of higher education and admissions testing, as well as more general articles dealing with broader issues in American higher education.

✌ 6 ✍

Student Financial Aid

The literature in the field of student financial aid has grown at a tremendous rate during the past four decades. This growth parallels the growth of the financial aid domain as a specialty profession within the student services field. When the financial aid functions of institutions were carried out as a minor responsibility of the admissions office or on a part-time basis by a member of the student affairs staff, very little was published about student financial aid.

By 1950 the concept of need-based financial aid had become popular, but aid tended to be disbursed based on the relatively simple basis of annual family income. After the College Entrance Examination Board established a uniform method of collecting information about parental financial resources and devised sophisticated methods and formulas to compute student need based on a variety of factors, the resulting research, policies, and discussions about these policies promoted a substantial increase in publications related to student financial aid. The use of this information also required more specialized knowledge by someone at the institutional level, and thus financial aid as a specialty area began to emerge.

The reaction to Sputnik in the late 1950s also influenced the field of student financial aid. To aid in the search for and development of talent, especially scientific talent, the National Merit Scholarship Program was established. The federal government became heavily involved in providing financial resources to both students and institutions to assist able students from lower socioeconomic levels to continue their education. The 1958 National Defense Education Act (NDEA) initiated the first federally supported student financial aid programs since the post-World War II GI Bill. The GI Bill and the NDEA grants and programs eventually evolved into the current Pell Grants, the Supplemental Educational Opportunity Grants, and the Perkins Loan Program. With these federally funded programs came complex policies and regulations regarding disbursement, along with extensive reporting procedures designed to ensure against misappropriation of funds or fraud.

Various states also established programs of student financial aid. Financial aid offices thus were provided a mix of federal, state, and institutional funds consisting of both grants and loans to distribute according to various stipulated regulations and in line with fair and ethical practices. The provision of governmental aid brought with it many political considerations, and financial aid officers along with others in higher education and the various organizations representing higher education began to undertake substantial lobbying efforts within the different legislative bodies.

As the number of financial aid specialists increased, the National Association of Student Financial Aid Administrators (NASFAA) was organized and became an important source of much of the literature in the financial aid field. NASFAA publishes books and monographs, as well as a professional journal. The agencies in the federal government concerned with student financial aid also began publishing monographs and handbooks dealing with issues and updated policies addressing the disbursal of federal funds. A substantial body of literature has thus been produced, as evidenced by the number of resources cited in this chapter, almost all of which have been published since 1980.

This current literature contains discussions of many different types of issues that have now developed within this field. Questions have been raised regarding the treatment of income in such occupations as farming or the military services, and the extent to which certain types of family assets should be "taxed" is debated. The long-term impact of loans on students' educational and career plans has become an important concern. Whether or not a generation of young people are being overly burdened in their futures by excessive educational loans is a major consideration. There is also the difficulty in determining what constitutes a proper mix of grants, loans, and student employment. Policies and practices regarding the collection of student loans represent yet another important issue.

With the urgent necessity for many institutions to maintain or increase their enrollment, the use of financial aid to attract students has become an integral part of the admissions process. This has raised many policy and ethics issues that are discussed in this literature, including to what extent are institutions now "buying" students? Questions regarding the optimal amount of student part-time employment also appear in the financial aid literature since on some campuses part-time employment is one of the responsibilities of the financial aid office. On many campuses student employment is considered an integral portion of the total financial aid "packages" developed for individual students.

Financial aid counseling for students and the necessary policies and practices that accomplish this function are also discussed in the literature. Accompanying this is the complaint that although many agencies feel this is an important part of their responsibility, they are not accomplishing it due to all of the other demands already placed upon their inadequately staffed operations.

These important policies and issues in the field are discussed in the resources briefly enumerated in this chapter and in professional journals. By far the most important source of periodical literature in this field is the *Journal of Student Financial Aid* (no. 334). Since significant aspects of the financial aid field are important in the college admission process, the *Journal of College Admissions* (no. 271), the *College Board Review* (no. 273) and *College and University* (no. 272), often contribute articles relevant to this field as well.

Continually changing governmental regulations, the computerization of financial aid records, and the increasing complexity of the financial aid processes have led to the ever increasing specialization of this field. Increasing specialization leads to increasing isolation from others in the student services field, and this isolation is echoed in the literature of the field. The majority of student financial aid literature now appears only in those sources that deal either with financial aid alone or as related to admissions. Communication with other student services professionals and within the broader field of higher education through a wider range of literature is needed if this specialty is to be understood by other constituencies in higher education.

The references in this chapter begin with those related to the administration of financial aid programs and are followed by those dealing with student financing of higher education. These are followed by references concerned with governmental programs, student loan policies, and student employment. The concluding section contains references to several monographs regarding the student financial aid profession.

Administration

274 Binder, Shirley F. (ed.). *Responding to Changes in Financial Aid Programs.* New Directions for Student Services, no. 12. San Francisco: Jossey-Bass, 1980. 102 pages.

The challenges facing institutional aid administrators to provide access and choice to low- and middle-income students are increasing with the changes in federal laws and regulations. This sourcebook addresses the processes, research potentials, and strategies necessary to meet these challenges.

275 Clark, Robert B. (ed.). *Handbook for Use in the Preparation of Student Expense Budgets.* Washington, D.C.: National Association of Student Financial Aid Administrators, 1977. 140 pages.

This monograph provides a methodology for the construction of student budgets to be used in the calculation of financial aid needs. It provides the information for this purpose and is now used in conjunction with an update published in 1984 entitled *Constructing Student Expense Budgets.* (See entry no. 304.)

276 Collins, J. Stephen. *Student Financial Assistance: A Program for the Department of Education Audit Guide.* Washington, D.C.: National Association of Student Financial Aid Administrators, 1984. 69 pages.

This volume provides assistance to institutions in meeting the requirements for the auditing of federally supported student aid programs. It contains a lengthy checklist of compliance requirements for both general administration and for specific federal student aid programs.

277 El-Khawas, Elaine. *Management of Student Aid—A Guide for Presidents.* Washington, D.C.: American Council on Education, 1979. 27 pages.

This guide was prepared for senior administrators in colleges and universities to assist them in understanding the magnitude and impact of student aid in their institutions and to foster sound management principles for administering this aid on their campuses. Chapters deal with the presidential responsibilities for financial aid and the importance of the effective implementation and management of campus student aid policies.

★278 Fenske, Robert H.; Huff, Robert P.; and Associates. *Handbook of Student Financial Aid: Programs, Procedures, and Policies.* San Francisco: Jossey-Bass, 1983. 508 pages.

This book contains a number of chapters written by knowledgeable professionals and is designed to present the primary functions, policies, and programs for the delivery of student financial aids. The book provides considerable detailed information on the delivery of financial aid to students, including the dissemination of aid formation, determining financial need, packaging of awards, and disbursing funds. Financial aid policies and organizational structures for effective administration of financial aid programs are also provided.

★279 Henry, Joe B. (ed.). *The Impact of Student Financial Aid on Institutions.* New Directions for Institutional Research, no. 25. San Francisco: Jossey-Bass, 1980. 110 pages.

This sourcebook comprehensively examines the role of financial aid in institutional management. Featured are discussions regarding the impact of financial aid on enrollment and student achievement, the use of financial aid as a marketing tool, and ways of identifying student need and coordinating aid programs.

280 Keene, Roland; Adams, Frank C.; and King, John E. (eds.). *Money, Marbles, or Chalk: Student Financial Support in Higher Education.* Carbondale, Ill.: Southern Illinois University Press, 1975. 343 pages.

This often cited reference contains the contributions of thirty professionals in the fields of student financial aid and higher education and was designed to fill the need for a comprehensive publication on student financial aid. Chapters deal with the descriptions, philosophy, and administration of student financial assistance programs and the professional careers of those in student financial aid work.

281 National Association of Student Financial Aid Administrators. *Institutional Guide for Financial Aid Self-Evaluation.* (4th ed.) Washington, D.C.: National Association of Student Financial Aid Administrators, 1981. 95 pages.

This monograph is designed as a tool to assist financial aid administrators in evaluating the effectiveness of their financial aid programs as well as determining compliance with federal laws and regulations. It consists primarily of an extensive series of checklists regarding various aspects of financial aid in which brief statements of required or recommended practices are accompanied by a space to check either yes or no if that practice is being accomplished.

282 Office of Student Financial Assistance. *The Use of Automated Data Management in the Institutional Delivery of Student Financial Aid.* Washington, D.C.: Office of Student Financial Assistance/U.S. Department of Education, 1983. 129 pages.

This monograph provides aid to institutions in their conversion to an automated system of student financial assistance programs. Chapters describe the need for automation in financial aid management and outline the elements, implementation, and support of a data processing system. Over half of the monograph is made up of appendices containing a glossary of data processing terms and requirements for financial aid data processing systems.

283 Office of Student Financial Assistance. *Quality Control in the Institutional Delivery of Student Financial Assistance.* Washington, D.C.: U.S. Department of Education, 1984. 158 pages.

This monograph encourages the implementation of quality control programs in student financial aid organizations and provides information to assist in the establishment of such a program for institutional use. Chapters deal with the design, implementation, and evaluation of quality control programs, and an appendix includes a sample of such a program along with sample checklists, flowcharts, and a bibliography.

284 Office of Student Financial Assistance. *Statistical Sampling Handbook for Student Aid Programs.* Washington, D.C.: Office of Student Financial Assistance/U.S. Department of Education, 1984. 101 pages.

This monograph represents a basic sampling theory and statistics text applied to student financial aid. It includes relevant formulas and numerous sample applications in financial aid.

285 Van Dusen, William D. *A Design for a Model College Financial Aid Office.* New York: College Entrance Examination Board, 1980. 81 pages.

This monograph, a revision of two earlier editions by this author, briefly describes functions, administration, and organization of the financial aid office and its relationships both within the institution and with off-campus agencies.

Business and Accounting Aspects
of Financial Aid Programs

286 Office of Audit of the Inspector General. *Audit Guide — Student Financial Assistance Programs.* Washington, D.C.: U.S. Department of Education, 1984. 58 pages.

This manual is a guide for independent public accountants in their auditing of student financial assistance programs. It outlines general compliance requirements for the financial reporting, fiscal procedures, and record keeping regarding student eligibility, disbursements, and refund payments. Audit procedures for each of the specific types of federally funded aid programs are also outlined.

287 Student Financial Assistance Program. *The Business Officer's Guide to Student Aid: Changes in the Guaranteed Loan Program.* Washington, D.C.: Office of Student Financial Assistance, 1981. 41 pages.

This monograph is one of a series developed by the National Association of College and University Business Officers and describes changes made in the guaranteed student loan program by various legislative acts of 1980 and 1981. It discusses how these changes should be implemented by institutions. It is particularly concerned with the processes used to determine expected family contributions in computing student loan needs.

288 Student Financial Assistance Program. *The Business Officer's Guide to Student Aid: Changes in the National Direct Student Loan Program.* Washington, D.C.: Office of Student Financial Assistance, 1981. 51 pages.

This monograph is one of a series developed by the National Association of College and University Business Officers describing a number of legislative and regulatory changes in the National Direct Student Loan Program and how these changes should be implemented on the campus. The effect of these changes on business and fiscal administrative and operational procedures is presented, along with the impact on accounting and record keeping procedures.

289 Student Financial Assistance Program. *The Business Officer's Guide to Student Aid: Changes in the Pell Grant, Supplemental Educational Opportunity Grant, and College Work-Study Programs.* Washington, D.C.: Office of Student Financial Assistance, 1981. 24 pages.

This monograph is one of a series developed by the National Association of College and University Business Officers and discusses changes in the different federally funded financial aid programs and the effect these changes have on business and fiscal administration procedures. Accounting, record keeping, and reporting procedures required by these changes are detailed in this publication.

290 Student Financial Assistance Program. *The Business Officer's Guide to Student Aid: The Financial Aid Audit.* Washington, D.C.: Office of Student Financial Assistance, 1981. 27 pages.

This monograph is one of a series developed by the National Association of College and University Business Officers and is designed to cover the entire audit process from the selection of an auditor through the preparation for the audit, as well as records reviewed by the auditor through the closing of the audit. Internal and external audits, internal accounting, and management controls are discussed.

291 Student Financial Assistance Program. *The Business Officer's Guide to Student Aid: Managing Student Financial Aid— Techniques for Business and Fiscal Officers.* Washington, D.C.: Office of Student Financial Assistance, 1981. 36 pages.

This monograph is one of a series developed by the National Association of College and University Business Officers and is designed to assist institutional business officers in administering federally funded financial aid programs. It offers an overview of the administrative problems involved in financial aid management.

292 Student Financial Assistance Training Program. *Managing Student Financial Aid: Techniques for Business and Fiscal Officers.* Washington, D.C.: Office of Student Financial Assistance, 1981. 36 pages.

This monograph discusses the planning, organizing, and managing of student financial aid functions in an environment of change and uncertainty. Techniques that institutions can use to help make the financial aid system run smoothly and effectively are presented.

Student Financing of Higher Education

293 Carter, Glenda F. *Financial Aid and Black Students.* Lanham, Md.: University Press of America, 1988. 62 pages.

In this volume the trend toward smaller amounts of aid available to financially needy students is discussed, particularly as it relates to black student enrollment in higher education. The impact on black students, who are particularly heavily dependent on financial aid, and on black colleges is presented, along with several alternatives to lessen this impact.

294 Case, Karl E., and McPherson, Michael S. *Does Need-Based Student Aid Discourage Saving for College?* New York: College Entrance Examination Board, 1986. 19 pages.

This monograph summarizes a longer technical report that examines the question of whether increasing government aid to college students has discouraged families from saving for higher education or participating as fully as they otherwise might in the labor force. The question is examined for different income levels, and strategies for reducing savings and labor disincentives in student aid are discussed.

295 College Entrance Examination Board. *College Opportunity and Public Assistance Programs: Ideas for Resolving Conflicts.* New York: College Entrance Examination Board, 1984. 18 pages.

This report is a manual for student aid administrators and others as they attempt to help public assistance recipients pursue secondary education. Strategies for resolving conflicts regarding Aid to Families with Dependent Children (AFDC) programs and those of the federal student aid programs are presented since conflicting rules can discourage AFDC recipients from attending college.

296 Dickmeyer, Nathan; Wessels, John; and Coldren, Sharon L. *Institutionally Funded Student Financial Aid.* Washington, D.C.: American Council on Education, 1981. 78 pages.

This book provides a brief introduction to the various aspects of institutionally funded financial aid programs. Student employment and work-study programs are also discussed

297 Downey, Cathy; Schwarzbach, Adrienne; and Spring, Ellen. *Everything You Wanted to Know About Financial Aid but Had to Wait in a Line Too Long to Ask.* Washington, D.C.: United States Student Association, 1983. 123 pages.

This monograph describes processes by which students can have an impact on student aid programs and describes the various aspects of student aid procedures, policies, and organization on a university campus.

298 Foose, Robert A., and Meyerson, Joe W. *Alternative Approaches to Tuition Financing — Making Tuition More Affordable.* Washington, D.C.: National Association of College and University Business Officers, 1986. 80 pages.

In this monograph various plans for funding and paying tuition are presented along with examples of each. Various types of prepayment plans, delayed payment plans, loan programs, and student employment programs are discussed. Other aspects included are pricing, employee discounts, credit card and electronic payment, and tuition planning models, along with the advantages and disadvantages both to the institution and to students and their families. An appendix presents lists of institutions utilizing each of the types of tuition financing programs.

299 Johnstone, D. Bruce. *Sharing the Costs of Higher Education.* New York: College Entrance Examination Board, 1986. 184 pages.

This book examines the costs of higher education and the way these costs are shared among students and parents, taxpayers, contributors from business, and alumni donors in England, Germany, France, Sweden, as well as in the United States.

300 Kramer, Martin (ed.). *Meeting Student Aid Needs in a Period of Retrenchment.* New Directions for Higher Education, no. 40. San Francisco: Jossey-Bass, 1982. 105 pages.

This volume provides practical suggestions for the most effective methods of utilizing limited student aid funds and explores ways of compensating for governmental budget cuts. Ways of packaging aid that maximize students' ability to meet costs are presented.

301 Moran, Mary. *Student Financial Aid and Women: Equity Dilemma?* Washington, D.C.: Association for the Study of Higher Education, 1986. 135 pages.

The purpose of this monograph is to point out major policy issues on student aid that affect women students. Suggestions to improve the participation of women in student aid programs are presented.

302 National Student Aid Coalition. *Closing the Information Gap: Ways to Improve Student Awareness of Financial Aid Opportunities.* Washington, D.C.: National Student Aid Coalition, 1985. 37 pages.

The primary concern of this monograph is that information on student aid programs often does not reach the individuals — disadvantaged, minority, and nontraditional students — who most need the aid. Recommendations concerning ways in which the provision of information to these groups can be improved along with examples of innovative programs to accomplish this are included.

303 Office of Student Financial Assistance. *Counselor's Handbook.* Washington, D.C.: U.S. Department of Education, 1981. 46 pages.

This handbook is designed to assist counselors in helping students apply for federal financial aid. The first chapter gives an overview of the five major sources of federal student aid, the second explains the grant application forms, and the third explains the student eligibility report. Sample forms are provided, and several different policies dealing with special conditions and circumstances are outlined.

KVCC KALAMAZOO VALLEY COMMUNITY COLLEGE LIBRARY

Determination of Need

304 National Association of Student Financial Aid Administrators. *Constructing Student Expense Budgets.* Washington, D.C.: National Association of Student Financial Aid Administrators, 1984. 42 pages.

Financial aid administrators will find assistance in this monograph in constructing student expense budgets. It describes general principles for budget construction, sets forth the various types of expenses that make up students' budgets, and suggests methodological approaches for determining and substantiating student budgets. It includes a lengthy table presenting budget items that are considered allowable, allowable with documentation, and those considered nonallowable.

305 National Association of Student Financial Aid Administrators. *Standards for the Verification of Information to Determine Financial Aid Eligibility.* Washington, D.C.: National Association of Student Financial Aid Administrators, 1984. 48 pages.

This monograph presents methods and procedures that have been developed to verify information related to student need. It presents agency roles and institutional policies and procedures for verification, policies for dealing with contradictory information, and sample documents used to verify different types of financial need items.

306 National Association of Student Financial Aid Administrators. *Use of Tax Returns and the Review of Documents Used to Establish Eligibility for a Need-Based Financial Aid.* Washington, D.C.: National Association of Student Financial Aid Administrators, 1984. 19 pages.

This monograph gives a brief description of income tax forms and their use and points out the data on them that can be used in verifying income reported by students and their families.

307 National Association of Student Financial Aid Administrators. *Professional Judgment in Need Analysis.* Washington, D.C.: National Association of Student Financial Aid Administrators, 1987. 35 pages.

This monograph is designed to assist financial aid administrators in those cases when adjustments in student need must be made. It includes lists of items to consider in examining student needs and resources and parental assets and income. It identifies a variety of situations where professional judgments regarding student need is appropriate.

Federal Programs and Regulations

★308 Office of Student Financial Assistance. *A Guide to Disbursement, Refund, and Repayment.* Washington, D.C.: Office of Student Financial Assistance, 1984. 74 pages.

This monograph summarizes U.S. Department of Education policies regarding institutional and recipient responsibilities regarding the disbursement and repayment of federally funded student aid. Policies regarding records, and documentation of disbursement of grants, loans, and work-study are included along with appendixes that include sample refund policies and sample case studies.

National Policies

309 Carnegie Council on Policy Studies in Higher Education. *Next Steps for the 1980s in Student Financial Aid: A Fourth Alternative.* San Francisco: Jossey-Bass, 1979. 255 pages.

This report describes the funding and distribution of the many aspects of student financial aid. On the basis of these findings a number of specific recommendations are made for improvements.

★310 College Scholarship Service. *An Agenda for the Year 2000.* New York: College Entrance Examination Board, 1985. 220 pages.

This publication compiles papers presented at four colloquia along with the statements of thirty-one reactors dealing with the future of student financial aid. The papers deal with the need for student financial aid, who pays and who should pay, and the future roles of financial aid administrators and scholarship services.

311 Gillespie, Donald A., and Carlson, Nancy. *Trends in Student Aid: 1963 to 1983.* New York: College Entrance Examination Board, 1983. 50 pages.

This monograph reports statistics on student aid, tracing its growth over twenty years. Trends and amounts of different types of aid — particularly federal aid — college class, family income levels, and other related data are compared over the twenty-year period, and a large number of figures and tables display these trends.

312 Nelson, Susan C. *Community Colleges and Their Share of Student Financial Assistance.* New York: College Entrance Examination Board, 1980. 61 pages.

This monograph examines the distribution of participation in student financial aid programs in community colleges as compared with four-year institutions. Findings suggesting the underutilization of student aid programs, particularly those involving campus-based aid, are discussed, and a number of tables are included showing participation rates in various types of institutions.

313 Spero, Irene K. *The Use of Student Financial Aid to Attract Prospective Teachers: A Survey of State Efforts.* New York: College Entrance Examination Board, 1986. 27 pages.

This report surveys state-supported programs that seek to attract talented college students to teaching by providing a form of student financial aid that includes "forgiveness" schedules. The various types of programs are described, their effectiveness is discussed, and a brief description of programs operating in those states that have them are included in an appendix.

314 Stampen, Jacob O. *Student Aid and Public Higher Education: A Progress Report.* Washington, D.C.: American Association of State Colleges and Universities, 1983. 98 pages.

This report analyzes the distribution and impact of student financial assistance at public colleges and universities during 1981–82. It reports the characteristics of students who were the recipients of various types of student aid at these public institutions. The relationship of financial aid received to various costs was analyzed for both two-year and four-year public institutions.

315 Van Dusen, William D., and Higginbotham, Hal F. *The Financial Aid Profession at Work: A Report on the 1983 Survey of Undergraduate Need Analysis Policies, Practices, and Procedures.* New York: College Entrance Examination Board, 1984. 79 pages.

This monograph reports the results of a questionnaire survey of 2,000 institutions to determine current policies and procedures institutions follow in administering student aid programs. Subjects covered include need analysis policies and practices, verification and validation practices, policies and procedures regarding the packaging of aid, and practices regarding the awarding of no-need scholarships.

316 Washington Office of the College Board. *Who Receives Federal Student Aid?* New York: College Entrance Examination Board, 1986. 23 pages.

This monograph presents a number of graphs and tables of statistics comparing the different types of student financial aid received by students from different income categories and compares trends in this aid over the decade between 1973 and 1983.

Student Loans

317 College Scholarship Service. *Proceedings of the College Scholarship Service Colloquium on Student Loan Counseling and Debt Management.* New York: College Entrance Examination Board, 1986. 137 pages.

This publication contains four papers dealing with the implications of student borrowing, along with policies and procedures related to student borrowing and student loan counseling. It also contains the reactions of several financial aid professionals to the material presented in these papers.

318 Hansen, Janet S. *Student Loans: Are They Overburdening a Generation?* New York: College Entrance Examination Board, 1987. 40 pages.

This monograph examines the question of whether the heavy dependence on student loans is creating serious problems for individuals or society now that a third to a half of all undergraduates leaving school are in debt for their education. What is known and what is not known about this question are discussed, along with a comparison of U.S. policies with those of Sweden and Germany.

319 Hansen, Janet S., and Wolfe, Mark L. *Student Loan Guarantee Agencies and Their Financing.* New York: College Entrance Examination Board, 1985. 25 pages.

This monograph examines the Guaranteed Student Loan (GSL) and the Parent Loans to Undergraduate Students (PLUS), federal low-interest loan programs, and the state and private nonprofit agencies that administer these programs. State-by-state costs of administering these funds are also reported.

★320 McAlvey, Warren. *Student Loan Collection Procedures.* Washington, D.C.: National Association of College and University Business Officers, 1977. 184 pages.

This monograph contains an overview of student loan practices and procedures and then specifically covers direct student loans, guaranteed student loans, and student loans in the various health professions. A number of sample forms and letters are included.

321 National Association of Student Financial Aid Administrators. *Stages in the Development of a Financial Counseling and Debt Management Model.* Washington, D.C.: National Association of Student Financial Administrators, 1984. 29 pages.

This monograph is designed to assist financial aid administrators in counseling students regarding the debts they may incur in financing their postsecondary education. Portions of the monograph deal with the development of a financial counseling and debt management program, aspects of financial counseling during the undergraduate and postgraduation years, and includes loan repayment tables and graphs.

322 National Association of Student Financial Aid Administrators. *Loan Counseling, Requirements, and Good Practice.* Washington, D.C.: National Association of Student Financial Aid Administrators, 1987. 63 pages.

This monograph is designed to assist financial aid administrators in educating students about their indebtedness and helping them deal with the repayment of their loans, as well as assisting them to fulfill the conditions for loan counseling now prescribed by the federal government. It contains the legal requirements for loan counseling along with a decision-making model for an institutional program and useful references, sample forms, and checklists.

Student Employment

323 Christoffel, Pamela. *Working Your Way Through College: A New Look at an Old Idea.* New York: College Entrance Examination Board, 1985. 36 pages.

This monograph surveys federal, state, and institutional work-study programs. It examines recent trends in student employment, work-study, and cooperative education programs. The extent to which students use part-time and full-time employment to meet college costs is summarized for various types of institutions. Ways in which work-study and cooperative education programs can be enhanced to provide larger sources of support are proposed. An appendix that briefly describes the status of state work-study programs as of 1985 is included.

The Profession

324 Davis, Jerry S. *Characteristics of Directors of Financial Aid, Their Institutions, and Their Staffs, 1983–84.* Washington, D.C.: National Association of Student Financial Aid Administrators, 1984. 30 pages.

Information about financial aid administrators and their staffs was obtained from over 2,000 directors. The educational and work backgrounds, salaries, and sizes of staffs were obtained and compared among different types and sizes of institutions. Other demographic data regarding both the staff members and financial aid policies at the different institutions are also provided.

325 Davis, Jerry S. *The Members Appraise Their Association.* Washington, D.C.: National Association of Student Financial Aid Administrators, 1986. 124 pages.

Presented here are the results of an extensive survey of a random sample of 1,500 financial aid administrators regarding the programs and services that the National Association of Student Financial Aid Administrators offers to its members. Results are summarized in narrative form with the tabular data placed in an extensive appendix.

326 Grotrian, Harvey T.; Barber, Frank; Harris, Edwin B.; MacQueen, Betty L.; Martin, Dennis J.; Nelson, Daniel C.; Payton, Goldeau G.; Ulrichson, Ardys M.; and White, Gordon W. *A Profession in Transition: Trends in Financial Aid Administrator Characteristics and Attitudes, 1977–1987 and An Examination of Current Issues.* Ann Arbor: Midwest Association of Student Financial Aid Administrators, Office of Financial Aid, University of Michigan, 1987. 96 pages.

This monograph presents the results of a survey questionnaire received from 886 members of the Midwest Association of Student Financial Aid Administrators. It compares salary levels and staff sizes at institutions of various sizes with different types of control. It also reports considerable data regarding the characteristics of financial aid administrators, descriptions of their organizations, characteristics of the institutions where they work, their programs, and their attitudes. Aspects such as salaries and career satisfaction are compared by various characteristics of financial aid administrators and by institutional characteristics.

327 Midwest Association of Student Financial Aid Administrators. *A Profession in Transition.* Ann Arbor, Mich.: Midwest Association of Student Financial Aid Administrators, 1987. 96 pages.

In addition to the citation for this monograph listed in entry no. 326, this resource is also found referenced under the above citation. The full title and description of this monograph are found in entry no. 326.

328 Morris, Stephen A. *MASFAA Pioneer and Leader.* West Lafayette, Ind.: Midwest Association of Student Financial Aid Administrators, 1987. 139 pages.

This monograph summarizes the development of the Midwest Association of Student Financial Aid Administrators from its inception to the present. Included are the reactions of a profession to various federal student financial aid initiatives. Approximately the last two-thirds of the publication is an appendix that summarizes the programs and business of the association likely to be of interest primarily to professionals in the Midwest.

Periodicals and Annuals

329 *College Scholarship Service Need Analysis: Theory and Computation Procedures for the 1985–86 FAF.* Annual publication of the College Entrance Examination Board, 45 Columbus Avenue, New York, N.Y. 10023.

This manual is published annually by the college board for use in analyzing student need with the College Scholarship Service's financial aid form. It covers the theory of need analysis and the measurement of parental ability to pay along with computation procedures using data on the form, procedures for processing the form, the packaging of student aid, and its use with special problems in need analysis.

★**330** *Current Title IV Regulations.* Published continuously by the Office of Student Financial Assistance, U.S. Department of Education, 400 Maryland Avenue SW, Washington, D.C. 20202.

Those regulations dealing with student financial aid that appear in the *Federal Register* are published continuously by this office and are designed to be stored in a loose-leaf notebook. This resource thus provides the basis regulations for the administration of federal student financial assistance programs.

331 *Encyclopedia of Student Financial Aid.* Published and continuously updated by the National Association of Student Financial Aid Administrators, 1920 L Street NW, Suite 200, Washington, D.C. 20036.

This resource of federally supported financial aid programs is published in the form of a very thick loose-leaf binder to which additional information and updates and changes are added as they appear. Programs and regulations are described in language more easily understood by financial aid administrators than in the formal publications of the federal government. The encyclopedia is divided into six sections dealing with the various federal programs such as the Pell Grants, the Supplemental Educational Opportunity Grants, and the Perkins Loan Program. The encyclopedia and the subscription to continuous updates is available from the National Association of Student Financial Aid Administrators.

★332 *Federal Student Financial Aid Handbook.* Annual publication of the Office of Student Financial Assistance, U.S. Department of Education, 400 Maryland Avenue SW, Washington, D.C. 20202.

This handbook is published annually in separate chapters dealing with policies and procedures related to the various federal financial aid programs. In addition to including current policy changes and changes for the various programs, it also includes worksheets and sample cases.

333 *Handbook for Financial Aid Administrators.* Annual publication of the American College Testing Program, P.O. Box 168, Iowa City, Iowa 52243.

This manual is published annually dealing with the use of ACT's student need analysis surveys. It includes policies and procedures in computing student need, utilizing data from the several forms containing parental and student financial resources. Included are calculations for sample cases and an appendix that contains numerous tables and a variety of answers to commonly asked questions about financial aid.

334 *Journal of Student Financial Aid.* Published three times a year by the National Association of Student Financial Aid Administrators (NASFAA), 1920 L Street NW, Washington, D.C. 20036.

This journal publishes articles of interest to those in the financial aid profession regarding the effective administration of student financial aid programs, the effective delivery of student financial assistance, and results of research projects. A subscription is included in membership to the National Association of Student Financial Aid Administrators.

335 *NASFAA Newsletter.* Published twice monthly by the National Association of Student Financial Aid Administrators, 1920 L Street NW, Washington, D.C. 20036.

This newsletter is published for NASFAA members to provide current information regarding the administration of student financial aid programs.

336 *National Membership Directory.* Annual publication of the National Association of Student Financial Aid Administrators, 1920 L Street NW, Washington, D.C. 20036.

This national membership directory is published annually, listing all the institutional members and their financial aid staff including names, titles, and phone numbers. Federal and state agencies and resources are also listed along with association officers, commissions, and committees.

❧ 7 ❧

Residence Life

On many college and university campuses, a student service exists that is often viewed as ancillary or peripheral to the institutional mission. That service is residence life, which is traditionally perceived as responsible only for the room and board of students. However, increasingly a philosophical stance has been adopted that challenges the assumption that learning is a product of only the classroom. Many factors outside the classroom influence learning, and residence services are increasingly being utilized as an integral part of the educational process. Regardless of the administrative intent, residence services have long functioned as centers of learning, where students are presented with the differing viewpoints and beliefs of other students, where idea exchanges can occur informally both in regard to the academic curriculum and other issues, and where adopted group standards are determined that serve as guides for behavior in the classroom and elsewhere.

Historically, residence facilities have been a part of American colleges and universities. Originally, since these institutions were based on the English college, they were correspondingly built in rural areas outside major cities, and therefore room and board needed to be provided for students.

During the nineteenth century the interest in and concern for adequate student housing waxed and waned during different decades. Finally, in the late 1920s, an interest in collegiate residence halls was rejuvenated due to the gifts of Edward S. Harkness, which established the house system at Harvard and the college system at Yale.

Federal money for higher education increased from the end of World War II to the mid 1960s, and loans were made available to build residence halls. Consequently, a great number were built to house the bulging population of students entering higher education during this era. Many of these were high-rise, cell-block style, with long hallways of rooms. Currently, with aging facilities a concern, many are now adopting suite design, halls with rooms sharing central areas, as these appear to lead to greater student satisfaction and less stress and vandalism.

Besides the responsibility of providing an environment conducive to learning for students, residence services oftentimes also provide support for extracurricular activities and programs, advising and peer counseling for residents, and primary interventions for many students experiencing emotional or academic difficulty. Although these services often exist as fundamental student services of the institution, there is not a great deal of current literature dealing with these subjects.

With the sheer number of persons on campuses who work within residence life and the role of this service on the campus, it is surprising to uncover so few current resources in the literature. A large number of books were written regarding this specialty in the 1950s, but there has been a significant decline in publications since. One reason for this is directly related to the persons who comprise the professional work force in this area. Typically, these professionals are younger and at the beginning of their careers. The services require considerable amounts of energy, much evening, weekend, and live-in work, and often result in rapid burnout. There is a tendency for individuals in these positions to either move out of them entirely or to move on to administrative posts. Many of the direct-service positions are open to individuals with little or no training in student development or are held by graduate students working on a part-time basis. These individuals are less likely to contribute to the scholarly literature of their field.

Residence life has come to be extremely broad in its service capacity and has changed dramatically in its philosophical orientation. Originally, food and housing were the primary functions and were provided within a clear structure of *in loco paren-*

tis. In the 1960s and 1970s the decrease of the parental attitudes and parietal rules contributed to an emerging sense of the student as a consumer of services. As housemothers were replaced with hall directors and resident assistants, there was increased reliance on the paraprofessional. Increasingly, these services and the efforts of paraprofessional staff became an important marketing tool for many institutions as enrollment levels declined.

After World War II, with the increased enrollment of married students due to the GI Bill, residence services also expanded to include married student and family housing facilities. At many institutions, this extended to apartment housing for single students as well, so that individuals may have a choice of traditional residence halls or apartment-style dwellings. As studies focused on student satisfaction, the traditional residence hall also changed, and additional services such as educational programming, fitness centers, photography darkrooms, semi-private kitchenettes, or special-interest houses were provided.

The literature available is practitioner-oriented and therefore often found in the form of journal articles supported by professional associations within the specialty areas of residence services. It is also broad in scope with literature addressing topics as far-reaching as staff training, roommate compatibility, physical facilities, pest control, educational programming, food preparation, and suicide prevention. The result has been limited numbers of theoretical or philosophical articles or monographs in this area. A good source of information for literature more theoretical in nature and applicable to this specialty can be found in Chapter Three on student development. Certainly, Arthur Chickering's work on vectors of student development (see entry no. 45) and the environmental theorists discussed in Chapter Three have had an impact on this specialty.

As for the research dealing with residence life, this field is unique in its ready access to a large portion of the student body. Typically, residence hall students are a captive audience for studies, and consequently there exist a great number of studies in a variety of journals, on issues as widely varying as roommate choices and personal development. Within this bibliography, little effort has been made to include the scope of articles available within this field. However, the *ACUHO-I Bibliography on Residence Halls* (1987, no. 337) is an excellent source covering the breadth of articles available. Suffice it to say that journals ranging from the counseling profession to architecture, to the specialty area of residence or food services, all at one time or another contain articles pertinent to this field. Some of the journals that feature related articles are listed as a suggested starting point for those interested in this area.

Over the years the *Journal of College Student Development* (no. 1) has been the primary source for journal articles related to residence life. More recently, the *Journal of College and University Student Housing* (no. 366) has emerged as another important source of housing literature. The *NAWDAC Journal* (see entry 2) and the *NASPA Journal* (see entry 3) are also significant sources of periodical literature regarding student housing.

General

★337 Blimling, Gregory S.; Gehring, Donald D.; Gibson, Thomas; Grimm, James C.; Schuh, John H.; and Mc-Kinnon, William. *An ACUHO-I Bibliography on Residence Halls.* Columbus, Ohio: Association of College and University Housing Officers-International, 1987, 468 pages.

This publication is a general list of the majority of reference material available on the general topic of residence halls dating from the 1800s to more current publications. The material is organized into ten categories: historical development; financing; planning, construction and facilities; organization and administration; programming; personnel; educational development; food service; legal issues; and miscellaneous areas of interest. Materials included encompass books, periodicals, monographs, newspaper articles, ERIC documents, dissertations and theses,

and proceedings of annual conferences. This is an excellent
source to begin with in researching an area of residence life.

Administration

338 Blimling, Gregory S., and Schuh, John H. (eds.). *In-
     creasing the Educational Role of Residence Halls.* New Direc-
     tions for Student Services, no. 13. San Francisco:
     Jossey-Bass, 1981. 116 pages.

Community development, educational programming, and environmental management are explored in this volume, which
seeks to provide a framework for maximizing the development
of students in a residential setting. Issues such as the design
of the physical environment, the selection and training of staff,
and predictions for the future of residential life are also discussed.

339 Gehring, Donald D. (ed.). *Administering College and Univer-
     sity Housing: A Legal Perspective.* Asheville, N.C.: College
     Administration Publications, 1983. 108 pages.

This book covers many of the legal aspects regarding the administration of college housing operations. It provides a survey
of such constitutional protections for students as free speech,
organizations, search and seizure issues, contract and landlord
issues, and examines topics dealing with tort liability, negligence,
and risk management. Lists of legal sources, federal laws, and
relevant court cases are also included.

340 Huebner, Lois A. (ed.). *Redesigning Campus Environments.*
     New Directions for Student Services, no. 8. San Fran-
     cisco: Jossey-Bass, 1979. 108 pages.

Concepts of person-environment interaction are applied to
assessment and redesign of campus settings from the residence
hall to various student services and to the entire campus.

341 Moos, Rudolf H. *Evaluating Educational Environments: Procedures, Measures, Findings, and Policy Implications.* San Francisco: Jossey-Bass, 1979. 344 pages.

This book presents a framework for evaluating social environments and the development of inventories to aid in such evaluation. The first half of the book deals with college student living units, and the second with secondary school classrooms. The effects of living groups on student attitudes and behavior are discussed, and a chapter analyzing college student drinking patterns is also included.

342 Schneider, Lynette D. "Housing." In William T. Packwood (ed.), *College Student Personnel Services.* Springfield, Ill.: Thomas, 1977, pp. 125–152.

This chapter reviews the literature in the student housing field up to 1975. The chapter is organized into sections that address literature dealing with the rationale for student housing, administration and staffing of residence halls, and residence hall programs designed to supplement institutions' educational objectives. For a description of Packwood's complete work see entry no. 27.

Staff Development

343 Ender, Ken; Kane, Nancy; Mable, Phyllis; and Strohm, Meredith. *Creating Community in Residence Halls—A Workbook for Definition, Design, and Delivery.* Washington, D.C.: American College Personnel Association, 1980. 30 pages.

This workbook is designed to be used in the training of residence hall staff and assisting them to design and implement community development programs in the residence halls.

344 Ender, Steven C., and Winston, Roger B., Jr. (eds.). *Students as Paraprofessional Staff.* New Directions for Student Services, no. 27. San Francisco: Jossey-Bass, 1984. 111 pages.

For a description of this work see entry No. 163.

345 Reynolds, Edward, Jr.; Komives, Susan B.; and Mable, Phyllis. *Residence Education: A Career Beginning or a Career Path?* Alexandria, Va.: American College Personnel Association, 1983. 53 pages.

This monograph is designed as a workbook to be used as part of an in-service training program or for individual assessment. It presents the knowledge bases and motivation, skills, and personal goals needed to undertake a career in residence services.

346 Schuh, John H.; Shipton, William C.; and Edman, Neal. "Counseling Problems Encountered by Resident Assistants: An Update." *Journal of College Student Personnel,* 1986, *27,* 26–33.

This article summarizes current resident assistant concerns and trends that have been surveyed every three years over a twelve-year period at Indiana University.

347 Shipton, William C., and Schuh, John H. "Counseling Problems Encountered by Resident Assistants: A Longitudinal Study." *Journal of College Student Personnel,* 1982, *23,* 246–252.

This study examined the kinds of counseling problems encountered by resident assistants at a large midwestern university during the decade of the 1970s. Results indicated the relative stability of the nature and frequency of counseling problems encountered by resident assistants.

★348 Upcraft, M. Lee, with the collaboration of Guy T. Pilato. *Residence Hall Assistants in College: A Guide to Selection, Training, and Supervision.* San Francisco: Jossey-Bass, 1982. 281 pages.

This guide was developed as a general reference to be used by an institution to create more effective management in the residence halls and better overall residential environments. It includes information regarding the selection of resident assistants and a complete description of a training and evaluation program. This guide also includes recommendations for using the student manual, *Learning to Be a Resident Assistant* (no. 349), as a supplement to the training program.

349 Upcraft, M. Lee, with the collaboration of Guy T. Pilato and Dan J. Peterman. *Learning to Be a Resident Assistant: A Manual for Effective Participation in the Training Program.* San Francisco: Jossey-Bass, 1982. 174 pages.

This manual was designed as a supplement to the training program described in *Residence Hall Assistants in College* (no. 348). It includes an overview of students' development during college, the development of interpersonal skills, the application of group leadership skills, and examples of typical situations and how to confront them.

Student Development

350 Anchors, Scott; Schroeder, Charles; and Jackson, Smith. *Making Yourself at Home: A Practical Guide to Restructuring and Personalizing Your Residence Hall Environment.* Alexandria, Va.: American College Personnel Association, 1978. 50 pages.

This book is a guide to increasing student satisfaction and social interaction while reducing operating costs in residence halls by allowing students to personalize their rooms and corridors. A variety of ways in which this personalizing of individual and group spaces can be accomplished are presented.

351 Astin, Alexander W. *Four Critical Years: Effects of College on Beliefs, Attitudes, and Knowledge.* San Francisco: Jossey-Bass, 1977. 293 pages.

For a description of this work see entry no. 90.

352 Chickering, Arthur W. *Commuting Versus Resident Students.* San Francisco: Jossey-Bass, 1974. 150 pages.

This major national study of residential living is an example of research methods used to examine problems traditionally resolved on the basis of political or economical considerations. Chickering's general conclusion that residential campus living positively affects student development has serious implications for economic trends, equal opportunity in education, and administrative decision making.

353 DeCoster, David, and Mable, Phyllis. *Student Development and Education in College Residence Halls.* Alexandria, Va.: American College Personnel Association, 1974. 278 pages.

This edited volume contains chapters by well-known authorities in student residences and student affairs who provide a manual and reference for residence hall staff. The emphasis is upon the education and development of students in the residence halls and the ways that this can be encouraged by student and professional staff members in residence hall programs.

★354 DeCoster, David D., and Mable, Phyllis (eds.). *Personal Education and Community Development in College Residence Halls.* Alexandria, Va.: American College Personnel Association, 1980. 355 pages.

A continuation and update of the theories and practices presented by the authors in a previous book, this reference is geared toward residence hall staff. There are four main sections covering developmental philosophy, relationships within a community setting, the educational process, and future considerations.

355 Gelwick, L. E., and Wienstocks, R. "Managing the Environment for Older Students." In H. Kaiser (ed.), *Managing Facilities More Effectively.* New Directions for Higher Education, no. 80. San Francisco: Jossey-Bass, 1980, pp. 67-79.

This chapter focuses on ways to adapt facilities to more appropriately and effectively meet the needs of a new constituency of students. Specific recommendations are included, along with a presentation of important characteristics of an older population.

356 Lapidus, Jacalyn; Green, Susan K.; and Baruh, Elda. "Factors Related to Roommate Compatibility in the Residence Hall — A Review. *Journal of College Student Personnel,* 1985, *26,* 420-434.

This review of twenty-three research studies focuses on student characteristics or behaviors related to roommate compatibility. Studies were divided into the four categories of personality, values or attitudes, student backgrounds, and student living habits. Little success was reported in discovering factors that are clearly related to roommate compatibility, but the different studies, presented in summary tables, provide an extensive list of items and concerns for housing officers and future researchers.

357 Levin, Bernard H., and Clowes, Darrell A. "The Effect of Residence Hall Living at College on Attainment of the Baccalaureate Degree." *Journal of College Student Personnel,* 1982, *23,* 99-104.

This article summarizes a study of the effects of residence hall living and concludes that when certain important background factors are controlled, the impact of residence hall living is not as strong as previous studies have tended to indicate.

358 Riker, Harold C. "Residential Learning." In Arthur W. Chickering and Associates, *The Modern American College: Responding to the New Realities of Diverse Students and a Changing Society.* San Francisco: Jossey-Bass, 1981, pp. 672–688.

The author discusses the various uses of residence halls particularly the function of supporting the academic development of students. He describes six residence hall programs that he believes provide excellent educational programs because they offer opportunities for personal growth and enhance academic learning. He also describes the advantages to participants in the Elderhostel movement. For a description of Chickering's complete work see entry no. 85.

359 Solmon, L. C., and Gordon, J. J. *The Characteristics and Needs of Adults in Postsecondary Education.* Lexington, Mass.: Lexington Books, 1981. 155 pages.

This book examines a landmark study on adult students in postsecondary institutions conducted by J. W. C. Johnstone and R. J. Rivera in 1965, and provides important information for educators, including a section on the living arrangements of this population.

360 Upcraft, M. Lee. "Residence Halls and Campus Activities." In M. Lee Upcraft, John N. Gardner, and Associates, *The Freshman Year Experience: Helping Students Survive and Succeed in College.* San Francisco: Jossey-Bass, 1989, pp. 142–155.

This chapter emphasizes the role of residence halls in enhancing student success and promoting retention and personal development. The author discusses factors to be considered in assigning freshmen to residence units, as well as the staffing of residence halls. The benefits to freshmen of organized campus activities programming are also briefly discussed in this chapter. For a description of Upcraft and Gardner's complete work see entry no. 100.

361 Whiteley, J. M. "Extracurricular Influences on the Moral Development of College Students." In Louise McBee (ed.), *Rethinking College Responsibilities for Values*. New Directions for Higher Education, no. 31, San Francisco: Jossey-Bass, 1980, pp. 45–50.

The author is well-known for his landmark experimental study of the moral and ethical development of college students. In this chapter he discusses the possible effects of specific types of campus experiences. For a description of McBee's complete work see entry no. 67.

Periodicals

362 *American Institute of Architects (AIA) Journal*. A bimonthly publication of AIA, The Octagon, Washington, D.C. 20036.

This journal, designed primarily for those in the field of architecture, often features articles regarding housing design or space utilization.

363 *American School and University*. Published monthly by the Educational Division of North American Publishing, 401 North Broad Street, Philadelphia, Pa. 19108.

Formed by a merger of Educational Executives' Overview and American School and University, this journal focuses on facilities, purchasing, and business administration.

364 *College Student Journal*. A quarterly journal available from the following address: P.O. Box 8508, Spring Hill Station, Mobile, Ala. 36608.

For a description of this periodical see entry no. 138.

365 *Educational Record.* A quarterly publication of the American Council on Education, One Dupont Circle, Washington, D.C. 20036.

For a description of this periodical see entry no. 7.

366 *Journal of College and University Student Housing.* Published semiannually by the Association of College and University Housing Officers-International, 101 Curl Drive, Suite 140, Columbus, Ohio 43210–1195.

This journal features articles on current research, literature reviews, and other information for those involved in the student housing profession.

367 *Journal of Environmental Systems.* Published monthly by the Baywood Publications Company, 26 Austin Avenue, Amityville, N.Y. 11701.

This journal is concerned with the analysis, design, and management of environments and frequently features articles regarding residence halls.

368 *Journal of Personality and Social Psychology.* Published monthly by the American Psychological Association, 1400 North Uhle Street, Arlington, Va. 22201.

This journal addresses all areas of personality and social psychology, with an emphasis on empirical reports. There are three independently edited sections: attitudes and social cognition, interpersonal relations and group processes, and personality processes and individual differences.

369 *Planning for Higher Education.* Published quarterly by the Society for College and University Planning, 2026M, School of Education Building, University of Michigan, Ann Arbor, Mich. 48109–1259.

This journal contains articles dealing with considerations and models for all types of planning in higher education including enrollment, buildings and grounds, space allocation, financial, academic, and strategic planning.

370 *Restaurants and Institutions.* Published biweekly, Cahner's Plaza, 1350 E. Touhy Avenue, P.O. Box 5080, Des Plaines, Ill. 60017–5080.

This glossy-type periodical is directed toward both the financial and operational management of food services and restaurants.

371 *The Talking Stick* (formerly *ACUHO News*). Published eight times a year by ACUHO-I, 101 Curl Drive, Suite 140, Columbus, Ohio 43210–1195.

This publication reports programming ideas and staffing news and provides a report of ACUHO-I activities.

⽈ 8 ⽤

Academic Advising
and Learning Assistance
Programs

In most higher education settings, an overwhelming amount of frequently changing information exists regarding academic policies: graduation requirements, distribution or general education requirements, prerequisites, options for academic majors, and other important academic information. Since this type of information is not readily at hand for the typical undergraduate, someone on the campus, usually a faculty member, is assigned to each undergraduate to review the academic progress of the student and to assist the student in making academic decisions. Academic advising in colleges and universities in this country has primarily consisted of a faculty member assigned to a group of undergraduates with the singular function of assisting the student in the selection and scheduling of courses.

This traditional system of providing academic advising has often been found wanting, particularly on the larger campuses. In those institutions where research and/or service is emphasized, academic advising is typically not a high-priority activity for faculty members. Their interests are centered around their own academic field, and they are less interested in advising undergraduates, especially the entering undergraduate or the undecided student. Even those institutions that place a high priority on teaching usually reward excellent classroom teaching

151

to a far greater extent than excellence in individual advising sessions. Furthermore, the educational and occupational "maps" have become much more complex, compounding the number of options available, prerequisites, requirements, programs within majors, graduate and professional school requirements, requiring knowledge beyond that of all but the most interested, conscientious, and experienced faculty adviser.

Some institutions have dealt with this concern by establishing formal or informal training programs for academic advisers. The first section of this chapter addresses these types of programs and research-based strategies for academic advisers. Other institutions make an effort to get the required information into the hands of advisers through newsletters, advising handbooks, and, most recently, computer software. On some campuses advising is now evolving into a more comprehensive process of academic, career, and personal development and is being performed by other professionals on the campus in addition to and in conjunction with faculty advisers. Other campuses have established specialized advising services in which full- or part-time academic advisers offer an organized office or program of academic advising. These changes have resulted from the need for earlier and better academic planning, the increasing diversity of students on the college campus, some of the recent social and economic conditions, and the concern about student attrition. The availability of computers to provide computer-based scheduling and computer-assisted advising have also influenced this evolution of academic advising programs. The literature thus contains volumes that present different types of systems of academic advising, including those that provide more coordination and increased evaluation of their effectiveness. The second section of the chapter focuses on advising by faculty and ways to enhance the process for both faculty and students.

By providing specialized advisement, it is believed that more competent advising—particularly for undecided students—will result. With at least a third of the students who enter four-year colleges essentially undecided regarding an academic major and perhaps an additional third of those who come decided changing their major one or more times during the four undergraduate years, it is important that academic advisers recognize the developmental process that students undergo in making educational and vocational decisions. It is also important that advisers be familiar with the process and with the appropriate referral agencies on the campus where undecided students may seek additional help.

Students have often complained that they have not received adequate academic advising, and this seems to be related to student attrition. With the current emphasis on recruiting and then maintaining those students on whom considerable resources have already been spent, increasing the competence of advising is seen as one important way to reduce student attrition and therefore maintain enrollments. With complaints about academic advising coming from both alumni and dropouts, renewed efforts have been undertaken on the part of various institutions.

As more older students return to the campus and utilize programs designed for continuing education and distance education, the need for academic advising becomes even more important. Most of these students have full-time responsibilities and spend relatively little time on the campus when not in class. Thus they do not pick up the information that residential students often learn through their informal contacts. These older commuting students have a need for a particular individual adviser or mentor on the campus to assist them in their educational planning, as well as to be available beyond the usual eight-to-five working hours. As the number of these students continues to increase, the need for professional educational advisers who are cognizant of the needs of such students will undoubtedly increase.

It is apparent from the literature reviewed in this chapter that advising programs vary greatly among institutions and that different approaches are appropriate for different institutions. It is also apparent that academic advising is receiving increased emphasis on many campuses, in regard to both the retention and recruitment of students and the renewed emphasis on the total development of the student. This emphasis will undoubtedly result in increased budgets and staff for professional advising programs and increased credit for advising for faculty, salary, and promotion decisions (Grites, 1979, no. 377).

Academic advising is a student service where academic affairs and student affairs meet. The formal advising programs that exist on some campuses often involve considerable collaboration between academic personnel and student services personnel. Because of such programs, some academicians on the campus are becoming increasingly aware of the concepts and theories of student development. The joint concerns regarding academic advisement by both academic affairs staff and student services staff can be seen by the two national associations that represent the field of academic advising: the National Academic Advising Association (NACADA) and the Association of College Academic Affairs Advisers (ACAFAD). NACADA tends to draw its members from the academic side of the campus but also includes a number of student services professionals. ACAFAD is a commission of the American College Personnel Association, which is itself a division of the American Association for Counseling and Development. Thus it tends to include more professionals who received their training in student services but includes many academicians as well. Through this collaboration in the area of academic advising, considerable progress may be made by student services staff in promoting the concept of student development.

The remaining sections of this chapter contain information for specific student needs. Many athletic departments have found it necessary to provide specialized academic advising for their athletes as well as to provide other educational services dealing with study skills, reading comprehension, and assistance with mathematics. Institutions have found similar needs among minority students, and special programs have been established for students who are underprepared academically for college and university academic competition. When the attitude existed that all students by reason of their admission were qualified to undertake academic work and those who were not qualified did not belong on a college or university campus, it was not seen as important to provide assistance in educational skills. With the arrival of various groups of minorities, handicapped students, and other special populations on the campuses, special assistance in the form of educational services, academic advising, tutoring, workshops, and other programs have been found to be necessary in order for such students to be able to remain enrolled. While there is still controversy about the role of institutions of higher education in providing such assistance, the establishment of a variety of different types of educational support services has provided the beginning of a body of literature dealing with these services. Again, the literature listed here is for professional staff in the field and does not include the many how-to books (for example, *How to Succeed in College, How to Be a Winning Student,* and so on) aimed at the general population.

Academic Advising Programs

372 Abel, Janice. "Academic Advising: Goals and a Delivery System." *Journal of College Student Personnel,* 1980, *21,* 151–155.

In this article the organization and coordination of an academic advising system is described, and a delivery system is presented and related to student development objectives.

373 Crockett, David S. *Academic Advising Audit.* Iowa City, Iowa: American College Testing Program, 1988. 172 pages.

This monograph is designed to assist institutions in evaluating their academic advising programs. It includes forms and materials to obtain information about these programs, as well as rating forms and evaluation materials designed to assess their effectiveness. Also included are the results of a national survey on academic advising and the Council for the Advancement of Standards (CAS) Standards and Guidelines for Academic Advising Programs and the CAS Guide for Evaluating Programs using the CAS standards.

374 Crockett, David S. (ed.). *Advising Skills, Techniques, and Resources.* Iowa City, Iowa: American College Testing Program, 1988. 881 pages.

This very large volume contains a wide variety of information and materials related to academic advising. It contains reprints of journal articles, book chapters, ACT materials, and examples of advising materials and adviser training programs. The material comes from a wide variety of sources, and much of it can be very useful to those responsible for academic advising programs. Because of the variety and amount of materials in this volume, it is not always easy to locate the desired resources found within this massive volume.

375 Gordon, Virginia. "Training Academic Advisers: Content and Method." *Journal of College Student Personnel,* 1980, *21,* 334–340.

Concepts and functions of academic advising programs are described, and five important elements of an adviser training program are presented.

376 Gordon, Virginia N. *The Undecided College Student: An Academic and Career Advising Challenge.* Springfield, Ill.: Thomas, 1984. 125 pages.

This brief volume reviews the literature on undecided students and the different types of centers and programs designed to meet their needs. The needs of various subgroups of undecided students are discussed and several model advising programs are described. A checklist for assessing current programs is also included.

377 Grites, Thomas J. *Academic Advising: Getting Us Through the 80s.* Washington, D.C.: American Association for Higher Education, 1979. 67 pages.

This report presents the historical development of academic advising, along with recommendations for improving existing services or for creating new academic advising systems. It includes an extensive bibliography.

★378 Habley, Wesley, R. (ed.). *The Status and Future of Academic Advising.* Iowa City, Iowa: American College Testing Program, 1988. 253 pages.

This edited volume contains eleven chapters by knowledgeable professionals in the field of academic advising. Chapters deal with the organization and delivery of advising systems, and the training, evaluating, and rewarding of academic advisers. Brief descriptions of exemplary academic advising programs are included, and the last chapter lists a number of annotated references dealing with this subject.

379 Kramer, Gary L., and Spencer, Robert W. "Academic Advising." In M. Lee Upcraft, John N. Gardner, and Associates, *The Freshman Year Experience: Helping Students Survive and Succeed in College.* San Francisco: Jossey-Bass, 1989, pp. 95–107.

The authors address the problem of identifying the academic advising needs of freshmen and discuss various programs to meet these needs. They discuss the use of computers in academic advising and the responsibilities of faculty advisers. For a description of Upcraft and Gardner's complete work see entry no. 100.

380 Winston, Roger B., Jr.; Ender, Steven C.; and Miller, Theodore K. (eds.). *Developmental Approaches to Academic Advising.* New Directions in Student Services, no. 17. San Francisco: Jossey-Bass, 1982. 114 pages.

This sourcebook examines academic advising from a student development perspective. It includes an overview of theoretical foundations, delivery system approaches, process evaluation, training procedures for advisers, and methods of advising special populations.

381 Winston, Roger B., Jr.; Miller, Theodore, K.; Ender, Steven C.; Grites, Thomas, J.; and Associates. *Developmental Academic Advising: Addressing Students' Educational, Career, and Personal Needs.* San Francisco: Jossey-Bass, 1984. 550 pages.

This book considers changes that have occurred in academic advising practices over the past several decades and discusses current practices and programs and the different advising needs of different types of students. The authors draw on a nationwide survey of academic advising practices at over 750 institutions. Selections include a summary of current practices, strategies for advising special populations, use of various techniques and computers, organizational structures, adviser training, and examples of noteworthy programs.

Advising by Faculty

382 Kramer, Howard C., and Gardner, Robert E. *Advising by Faculty.* West Haven, Conn.: National Education Association, 1983. 56 pages.

This monograph is designed as a manual for faculty to read in order to better understand the various roles and responsibilities of faculty advising, to provide a model of the advising process, and to give examples of what happens in the advising relationship. Since the majority of faculty advising is informational in nature examples of informational resources are given, and ways to avoid communication problems are discussed. The importance of the adviser as an adult role model is also stressed.

383 Schein, Howard K.; Laff, Ned S.; and Allen, Deborah. *Giving Advice to Students: A Road Map for College Professionals.* Alexandria, Va.: American College Personnel Association, 1987. 130 pages.

This handbook for student advising gives various hints, techniques, and strategies. It is primarily aimed at academic and educational advising provided by faculty members but also includes dealing with certain counseling problems, such as distress, anxiety, and depression. Included is a practical scheme for assisting students in becoming self-advising and in developing career decision-making strategies and critical thinking skills.

384 Wilder, Jerry R. "A Successful Academic Advising Program: Essential Ingredients." *Journal of College Student Personnel*, 1981, *22*, 488–492.

This brief article gives the necessary ingredients for an adequate academic advising program composed of teaching faculty. It includes a discussion of the selection, training, evaluation, and reward system for successful academic advising.

Learning Assistance Programs

385 Brown, Wesley C. "College Learning Assistance: A Developmental Concept." *Journal of College Student Personnel*, 1982, *23*, 395–401.

This article examines the developmental learning theory that can underlie a learning assistance program (LAP) on a college campus and includes a model for such a program based on these principles.

386 Christ, Frank L., and Coda-Messerle, Margaret (eds.). *Staff Development for Learning Support Systems*. New Directions for College Learning Assistance, no. 4. San Francisco: Jossey-Bass, 1981. 108 pages.

This volume presents a variety of training models for learning assistance staff, which focus on developing versatile professional and paraprofessional staff so as to offset meager resources. The structure and function of learning assistance centers and specific personnel roles are delineated.

387 Lauridsen, Kurt (ed.). *Examining the Scope of Learning Centers*. New Directions for College Learning Assistance, no. 1. San Francisco: Jossey-Bass, 1980. 100 pages.

This examination of the history and the specific resource needs of learning assistance centers features a survey of centers in diverse settings and consideration of which skills programs appear to work best. An assessment of the effects of federal support and regulations on the continued growth of such centers is included.

388 Lauridsen, Kurt V., and Myers, Carmel (eds.). *Summer Programs for Underprepared Freshmen.* New Directions for College Learning Assistance, no. 10. San Francisco: Jossey-Bass, 1982. 111 pages.

This sourcebook examines summer programs designed for assisting underprepared freshmen in adapting to a campus environment. It includes an analysis of the diverse program models and recommends the best methods for student recruitment and testing, staff and resource use, and evaluation.

389 Lenning, Oscar, and Nayman, Robbie (eds.). *New Roles for Learning Assistance.* New Directions for College Learning Assistance, no. 2. San Francisco: Jossey-Bass, 1980. 105 pages.

This sourcebook provides a comprehensive look at the different ways that learning centers can assist students, faculty, and administrators. Emphasis is placed on the development of mutually beneficial alliances with faculty and other student services. An overall evaluation, to determine both financial and program effectiveness, concludes this volume.

390 Levine, Daniel, and Associates. *Improving Student Achievement Through Mastery Learning Programs.* San Francisco: Jossey-Bass, 1985. 300 pages.

Through case examples and other illustrations of successful programs, this volume addresses how to improve student performance through mastery learning. This method helps students to systematically master units of material through frequent feedback and reinforcement.

391 Roueche, John E. (ed.). *A New Look at Successful Programs.* New Directions for College Learning Assistance, no. 11. San Francisco: Jossey-Bass, 1983. 114 pages.

Through the analysis of effective programs already under way in diverse colleges and universities, this volume identifies the key features important in learning assistance programs.

392 Vaughan, George B., and Associates. *Issues for Community College Leaders in a New Era.* San Francisco: Jossey-Bass, 1983. 275 pages.

For a description of this work see entry no. 193.

393 Walter, Timothy L.; Gomon, Audrey; Guenzel, Pamela J.; and Smith, Donald E. P.: "Academic Support Programs." In M. Lee Upcraft, John N. Gardner, and Associates. *The Freshman Year Experience: Helping Students Survive and Succeed in College.* San Francisco: Jossey-Bass, 1989, pp. 108–117.

The authors identify academic weaknesses of freshmen and present five steps to establishing successful support programs. These academic assistance programs are designed to benefit all freshmen, not only those with academic deficiencies. For a description of Upcraft and Gardner's complete work see entry no. 100.

394 Walvekar, Carol (ed). *Assessment of Learning Assistance Services.* New Directions for College Learning Assistance, no. 5. San Francisco: Jossey-Bass, 1981. 123 pages.

An overview of all types of learning assistance programs, this volume addresses a range of approaches and evaluation procedures. The discussion includes evaluation of staff efficiency and quality, development of appropriate and flexible curricula, more sophisticated ways of assessing student capabilities, and innovative programming techniques.

Specific Learning Skills

395 Akst, Geoffrey (ed.). *Improving Mathematical Skills.* New Directions for College Learning Assistance, no. 6. San Francisco: Jossey-Bass, 1981. 137 pages.

A comprehensive discussion of the variety of aspects important to consider in the development of remedial programs, this volume investigates the sources of difficulty in mathematics for students and provides information on many remedial techniques.

396 Algier, Ann S., and Algier, Keith W. (ed.). *Improving Reading and Study Skills.* New Directions for College Learning Assistance, no. 8. San Francisco: Jossey-Bass, 1982. 99 pages.

This volume focuses primarily on practical ways to improve a variety of study skills, including reading, writing, note taking, time management, and work organization. Particular skills required in different disciplines are assessed, and methods for teaching these skills are presented. Innovative methods of remedial instruction and an examination of the role of faculty as study skills counselors are included.

397 Hawkins, Thom, and Brooks, Phyllis (eds.). *Improving Writing Skills.* New Directions for College Learning Assistance, no. 3. San Francisco: Jossey-Bass, 1981. 116 pages.

This volume provides an examination of how learning assistance centers are responding to the decline in writing ability among a broad spectrum of students. Different methods such as writing labs, which feature self-paced instruction, versus writing centers, which provide tutors, are discussed. Information is also included to assist in the development of a writing center, from funding and expansion to institute evaluation and accountability.

Assisting Special Populations

For key resources on special student populations see entries 102–114 in Chapter Three.

Underprepared Students

398 Cross, K. Patricia. *Beyond the Open Door: New Students in Higher Education.* San Francisco: Jossey-Bass, 1971. 200 pages.

In this book the author discusses the remedial and developmental education as well as different types of curriculum and instruction that will be needed as institutions adopt an open-door policy of admissions. She suggests individualized instruction, self-paced modules, and education for personal development and interpersonal skills. Appendixes include the results of a questionnaire regarding remedial services offered by American Community Colleges and the American College Personnel Association statement regarding the use of group experiences in higher education.

399 Cross, K. Patricia. *Accent on Learning: Improving Instruction and Reshaping the Curriculum.* San Francisco: Jossey-Bass, 1976. 291 pages.

This presentation of promising and innovative educational programs won the 1976 American Council on Education Book Award. Educational programs from over 1,000 studies are examined in detail, and a model of education is demonstrated that incorporates academic concerns with individual student differences.

400 Maxwell, Martha. *Improving Student Learning Skills: A Comprehensive Guide to Successful Practices and Programs for Increasing the Performance of Underprepared Students.* San Francisco: Jossey-Bass, 1979. 518 pages.

In this book the author presents a discussion of the organization, administration, staffing, policies, and procedures for organizing a program to assist students whose skills or abilities leave them unprepared for the competition they face in particular institutions or curricular programs. A rationale for providing such assistance, the types of programs and resources needed to provide it, and the competencies of the staff are discussed. Special learning needs and assessment techniques are presented, and a variety of sample resource materials are included.

401 Wilson, Lester (ed.). *Helping Special Student Groups.* New Directions for College Learning Assistance, no. 7. San Francisco: Jossey-Bass, 1982. 108 pages.

This sourcebook examines how learning assistance programs have contributed to the academic progress of students who have traditionally had limited access to higher education opportunities. Effective strategies are considered for a variety of student groups such as the physically handicapped, learning disabled, economically disadvantaged, students for whom English is a second language, and others.

Learning-Disabled Students

402 Biller, Ernest F. *Understanding and Guiding the Career Development of Adolescents and Young Adults with Learning Disabilities.* Springfield, Ill.: Thomas, 1985. 180 pages.

This publication offers an overview of assessment, exploration, and curriculum procedures for career development, with specific consideration of the career self-concept and implications of the learning disability for that self-concept.

403 Schmidt, Marlin R., and Sprandel, Hazel Z. (eds). *Helping the Learning-Disabled Student.* New Directions for Student Services, no. 18. San Francisco: Jossey-Bass, 1982. 107 pages.

This comprehensive guide to understanding the physical, psychological, social, and educational problems of learning-disabled students focuses on program development to address these concerns.

Handicapped Students

404 Laing, J., and Farmer, M. *Use of the ACT Assessment by Examinees with Disabilities.* Iowa City, Iowa: American College Testing Program, 1984. 33 pages.

Scores on the American College Testing Program Scholastic and Academic Aptitude tests were examined over a five-year period for students with visual and auditory disabilities and those with motor disabilities. High school grade point averages and ACT scores for students with disabilities who required special testing and for students with disabilities who did not require special testing were compared with those of other students, and differences between these groups were reported.

405 Penn, J. Roger, and Dudley, David H. "The Handicapped Students: Problems and Perceptions." *Journal of College Student Personnel,* 1980, *21,* 354–357.

The results of a survey of handicapped students provide information on the problem faced by such students and their perceptions of needed services.

406 Redden, Martha Ross (ed.). *Assuring Access for the Handicapped.* New Directions for Higher Education, no. 25. San Francisco: Jossey-Bass, 1979. 121 pages.

This sourcebook focuses on practical ways to reduce the architectural and policy barriers restricting enrollment and employment of handicapped persons. It includes a review of federal guidelines and institutional experience.

407 Sprandel, Hazel Z., and Schmidt, Marlin R. (eds.). *Serving Handicapped Students.* New Directions for Student Services, no. 10. San Francisco: Jossey-Bass, 1980. 98 pages.

This publication provides an examination of the needs of handicapped students and how student services professionals can meet those needs. Included is a discussion of federal regulations regarding the handicapped and what student services should do to conform to those regulations.

408 Willingham, Warren W.; Ragosta, Marjorie; Bennett, Randy E.; Braun, Henry; Rock, Donald A.; and Powers, Donald E. *Testing Handicapped People.* Needham Heights, Mass.: Allyn & Bacon, 1988. 223 pages.

In this book the authors report research findings for disabled people who take special administrations of college and graduate school admissions tests. Research studies dealing with the test results, their psychometric characteristics, their validity, and the admissions decisions that resulted are reported.

Student Athletes

409 Shriberg, Arthur, and Brodzinski, Frederick R. (eds.). *Rethinking Services for College Athletes.* New Directions for Student Services, no. 28. San Francisco: Jossey-Bass, 1984. 98 pages.

This sourcebook focuses on the myths of athletics and describes the need to develop special support programs that address the concerns of college athletes. The authors suggest how student services staff and athletic department staff can cooperate to meet these needs and concerns. Special counseling and tutoring programs designed to assist athletes, women, and minority students are discussed.

410 Whitner, Phillip A., and Myers, Randall C. "Academics and an Athlete: A Case Study." *Journal of Higher Education,* 1986, *57*(6), pp. 659–672.

This article provides an example of an educational program designed to help those student athletes who are marginally prepared for college academic work. The case study describes the series of diagnostic and educational procedures applied to one student athlete and the specific interventions that assisted him in improving his academic success.

Periodicals

411 *NACADA Journal.* Published semi-annually by the National Academic Advising Association, B507 Padelford Hall, University of Washington, Seattle, Wash. 98185. This journal contains information and research, discusses issues and sample programs, and reviews books dealing with student academic advising.

ᘒ 9 ᘒ

International
Student Services

Once the part-time responsibility of a faculty member or member of the student services staff, positions in foreign student advising now require the ability to respond to a wide range of responsibilities and the possession of a greatly increased knowledge base. The literature in this field reflects this emerging specialty and both the depth and breadth of knowledge required in such a position. Since specific training programs either at the undergraduate or graduate levels for this type of position are very few, this knowledge is typically acquired through on-the-job training. Useful resources in this field are therefore particularly important in meeting the needs of those who must acquire most of their knowledge while filling these positions.

Because foreign students bring with them many cultural values that distinguish them from native students, a certain amount of understanding and acceptance of diverse cultural backgrounds without the problem of cultural stereotyping is important for those who work with international students. An understanding of the specific problems faced by foreign students and some of the unique adjustments they must make is also a necessity for professionals in this field. Political events and other developments in students' home countries can also have an impact on foreign students' attitudes and behavior, and foreign student advisers can be more effective if they have at least a general idea of what is taking place in their students' countries.

Furthermore, knowledge of the many and varied immigration laws and regulations is crucial to adequately advise and assist international students. Foreign student advising also requires an understanding of the educational backgrounds of these students and an ability to determine who is admissible to various programs in the employing institution. Thus a knowledge of the secondary and postsecondary educational systems in many countries and the ability to accurately evaluate transcripts and other admissions materials becomes important. The evaluation of proficiency in English and the problems associated with learning English as a foreign language also represent areas of concern to those working with foreign students in colleges and universities in this country.

The literature in the field of foreign student advising and related aspects of international education is found in a wide variety of sources. The National Association for Foreign Student Affairs (NAFSA) has been particularly active in producing books and monographs specifically designed for the foreign student adviser. In addition to the resources produced by this organization, the NAFSA Newsletter (no. 463) is published eight times a year, containing brief articles and announcements of current information for foreign student advisers.

An additional area of expertise in the field of international education deals with providing information for American students studying abroad. A number of publications addressing this topic are published by commercial publishers and are designed to give information to students planning to study or travel abroad. Very few references can be found that are directed at staff in international education offices who advise these students.

A number of books, monographs, and periodicals from the field of comparative education often contain information useful for foreign student advisers. Several edited volumes and periodicals in this field contain numerous studies on topics of little interest to foreign student advisers but contain specific chapters that are very useful. Those that deal with secondary and postsecondary education in various countries are probably of most interest to foreign student advisers. There are also articles and monographs that deal with students from particular countries and aspects of their education in the colleges and universities in the United States.

A few authors have examined foreign students in this

country in regard to numbers from the variety of countries, types of institutions attended, types of undergraduate and graduate curricula in which they are enrolled, and their length of stay in the United States. Others have examined the policies or lack of policies on the part of the United States government and on the part of the over 3,000 colleges and universities in this country in regard to foreign student enrollment.

References in this chapter begin with several that examine policies regarding international students in this country, followed by sources of information for foreign student advisers and for foreign students themselves. Next, sources of information about international students and international education programs are found. The next section of references deals with immigration policies, and following that is found literature related to the issue of the employment of nonnative English-speaking teaching assistants — a practice on most large university campuses that results in considerable controversy. Many international education offices assist American students who wish to study and/or travel abroad, and references for the literature dealing with this topic and those related to cross-cultural education are found in the next sections. References concerning the professional development of the foreign student advising field and periodicals related to this field are found in this chapter's concluding sections.

International Education Policies

412 Eddy, John P., and Associates. *International Education and Student Development Application.* Venice, Calif.: Bergus, 1985. 81 pages.

This brief volume examines international education and international student programs in higher education. It includes a wide variety of subjects dealing with international education and makes recommendations regarding ways it benefits both higher education and society.

413 Goodwin, Craufurd D., and Nacht, Michael. *Absence of Decision: Foreign Students in American Colleges and Universities*. New York: Institute of International Education, 1983. 49 pages.

This monograph reports the findings of an interview study of issues surrounding the attendance of international students at institutions of higher education in the United States. Interviews were conducted with politicians, university administrators, members of governing boards, faculty, students, and members of local communities in three different states. Both positive and negative aspects of the many issues and questions related to this topic are discussed, and the lack of any long-range planning or overall policies on the part of either government agencies or individual institutions is identified.

414 Lulat, Y. G-M, Altbach, Phillip G., and Kelly, David H. *Governmental and Institutional Policies on Foreign Students: Analysis, Evaluation, and Bibliography*. Buffalo: Comparative Education Center, State University of New York at Buffalo, 1986. 114 pages.

This monograph discusses and summarizes the development of governmental and higher education institutional policies related to foreign students. The rationale for admitting foreign students and policy issues at both the local institutional level and the national level are presented.

Foreign Student Advising

★415 Althen, Gary. *The Handbook of Foreign Student Advising*. Yarmouth, Maine: Intercultural Press, 1983. 208 pages.

This volume presents information and advice from a seasoned professional foreign student adviser to a newcomer in that field. The author's philosophy regarding foreign student advising and his stands on various issues in the field are clearly presented. Numerous appendixes include useful information and points of view on different issues in the field.

416 Burak, Patricia A. *Crisis Management in a Cross-Cultural Setting.* Washington, D.C.: National Association for Foreign Student Affairs, 1987. 57 pages.

This monograph prepares those who work with foreign students for a variety of emergency situations in which it is important to consider cross-cultural differences. These include physical and mental health problems, personal crises such as political upheavals in their home countries, legal or financial crises, sex-related crises, or other concerns such as suicide or missing persons.

★417 National Association for Foreign Student Affairs. *Advisers' Manual of Federal Regulations Affecting Foreign Students and Scholars.* Washington, D.C.: National Association for Foreign Student Affairs, 1982. 120 pages.

This manual provides a description of immigration laws and regulations affecting the legal status of students. The limitations of each type of visa are described, along with regulations regarding school transfer, employment, and temporary absence from the United States.

418 Pyle, K. Richard (ed.). *Guiding the Development of Foreign Students.* New Directions for Student Services, no. 36. San Francisco: Jossey-Bass, 1986. 95 pages.

The special needs of the growing number of foreign students are addressed, with emphasis on activities to enrich their United States college experience. Special attention is also paid to professional guidelines regarding recruitment and admittance policies.

Information for Foreign Students

★419 Althen, Gary. *American Ways.* Yarmouth, Maine: Intercultural Press, 1988. 192 pages.

This book is designed to interpret American customs and culture to foreigners, particularly foreign students. Suggestions are made about how to respond to American customs and attitudes, both in the United States and when meeting Americans traveling abroad.

★**420** College Entrance Examination Board. *Overseas Educational Advisers' Manual.* New York: College Entrance Examination Board, 1987. 398 pages.

Published in a loose-leaf format and periodically updated at irregular intervals, this manual is designed to assist those overseas in advising students who plan to study in the United States. It includes information regarding establishing overseas advising centers and contains a great deal of information about American higher education and admissions information for foreign students. Considerable specific information is given in a number of appendixes, including forms and information sheets in readily reproducible formats.

421 Goldstein, Amy J. (ed.). *Applying to Colleges and Universities in the United States: A Handbook for International Students.* Princeton, N.J.: Peterson's Guides, 1987. 315 pages.

This reference book provides facts and figures about more than 3,000 colleges and universities in the United States. It is intended to be distributed abroad to students considering studies in this country. It is updated at irregular intervals of two or three years.

422 Hood, Mary Ann G., and Schieffer, Kevin J. (eds.). *Professional Integration: A Guide for Students from the Developing World.* Washington, D.C.: National Association of Foreign Student Affairs, 1983. 143 pages.

This collection of writings by different authors presents a variety of topics dealing with the problems of the professional integration of foreign students trained in this country and the education they receive. Chapters deal with such widely ranging topics as alumni networking, problems faced by women foreign students, developing a resource library, communication problems, and continuing education for the returned professional.

423 Packwood, Virginia M., and Packwood, William T. *Admissions Requirements for International Students at Colleges and Universities in the United States.* Fargo, N. Dak.: Two Trees Press, 1985. 292 pages.

This compendium of information provides facts regarding admission to over 2,000 colleges and universities in the United States.

Foreign Student Recruitment

424 Jenkins, Hugh M. (ed.). *Foreign Student Recruitment: Realities and Recommendations.* New York: College Entrance Examination Board, 1980. 62 pages.

This report by the National Liaison Committee on Foreign Student Admissions examined current recruiting activities and factors affecting foreign student recruitment. It recommends the establishment of a national centralized recruitment clearinghouse.

★425 Silny, Josef. *Handbook on Establishing an International Recruitment Program.* Princeton, N.J.: Peterson's Guides, 1988. 118 pages.

This monograph briefly describes the steps necessary to establish a program for recruiting international students, with particular emphasis on developing and distributing informational materials. Approximately two-thirds of the publication is devoted to listing the addresses of overseas educational advising centers.

Foreign Student Characteristics

426 Barber, Elinor G. (ed.). *Foreign Student Flows.* New York: Institute of International Education, 1985. 129 pages.

This monograph summarizes papers presented by various authors at a conference on foreign students. Considerable data are presented regarding the flow of foreign students from various countries in the world. The fields in which they study and the cost concern are summarized, both in the text and in a number of tables and graphs. A great deal of statistical information dealing with foreign students is contained in this relatively brief monograph.

427 Boyan, Douglas R. (ed.). *Profiles: The Foreign Student in the United States.* New York: Institute of International Education, 1983. 138 pages.

This monograph contains the results of a biennial survey of U.S. institutions of higher education regarding their foreign students. This edition provides a description of the foreign student population in the United States, including information on field of study, academic level, gender, and age of students from each particular country.

428 Goodwin, Craufurd D., and Nacht, Michael. *Foreignness and Frustration: The Impact of American Higher Education on Foreign Students with Special Reference to the Case of Brazil.* New York: Institute of International Education, 1984. 51 pages.

This monograph reports the results of interviews conducted with a number of Brazilian alumni of American institutions, in a variety of careers. Their reactions to the education they received as well as to American society as a whole is discussed. The usefulness of the training they received and methods by which it could be increased are also presented. The results reported could be generalizable to students from many other countries.

★429 Lee, Motoko Y.; Abd-ella, Mokhtar; and Burks, Linda A. *Needs of Foreign Students from Developing Nations at U.S. Colleges and Universities.* Washington, D.C.: National Association for Foreign Student Affairs, 1981. 179 pages.

This monograph reports the results of a national study to assess the needs of foreign students from developing nations who are studying in academic degree programs in American postsecondary institutions. The report follows the general format of a Ph.D. dissertation and includes many of the results in tabular form. Results point out the most important and least important needs of foreign students, along with the extent to which these needs are satisfied by the educational programs and institutions in which these students study.

430 Meleis, Afaf I. "Arab Students in Western Universities." *Journal of Higher Education,* 1982, *53* (4), 439–447.

This article briefly describes aspects of cultures and educational systems in the Arab world that cause problems as these students adjust to higher education in this country. Strategies to help these students adapt are suggested.

431 Solmon, Lewis C., and Young, Betty J. *The Foreign Student Factor: Impact on American Higher Education.* New York: Institute for International Problems, 1987. 95 pages.

This monograph uses national data collected in the annual Cooperative Institutional Research Program to compare the characteristics, goals, and attitudes of foreign students with those of American students. The reasons that students selected the institutions that they did, the academic success of the students, and data regarding career and job aspirations are also compared for foreign students and their American counterparts.

432 Story, Kathryn E. "The Student Development Professional and the Foreign Student: A Conflict of Values?" *Journal of College Student Personnel,* 1982, *23,* 66–70.

The conflict between American values inherent in several of the different theories of college student development and those of foreign students from diverse cultural backgrounds are discussed.

International Education Programs

★433 Backman, Earl L. (ed.). *Approaches to International Education.* New York: Macmillan, 1984. 356 pages.

This book presents seventeen case studies of a variety of different types of international education programs in a wide variety of higher education institutions. Programs presented include those for foreign students, American students going abroad, institutional linkages between American and foreign universities, faculty exchanges, developmental assistance programs, and international education programming on the campus.

434 Barrett, Ralph P. (ed.). *The Administration of Intensive English Language Programs.* Washington, D.C.: National Association for Foreign Student Affairs, 1982. 109 pages.

This monograph discusses a number of important considerations in establishing and managing a program in the English language for international students. Considerations involved in selecting, teaching, evaluating, and advising students in such programs are covered, along with the management of students and faculty in these programs. In addition, several model programs with differing goals are outlined.

★435 Jenkins, Hugh M., and Associates. *Educating Students from Other Nations: American Colleges and Universities in International Education Interchange.* San Francisco: Jossey-Bass, 1983. 362 pages.

This analysis of the interchange process examines a range of problems and issues addressing American colleges and universities and the foreign students who attend them. With chapters by twelve authors ranging from recruitment and admissions to realizing the potentials of international educational interchange, this publication of the National Association for Foreign Student Affairs (NAFSA) demonstrates ways to organize a network of programs and services for international students.

436 King, Nancy, and Huff, Ken. *The Host Family Survival Kit: A Guide for American Host Families.* Yarmouth, Maine: Intercultural Press, 1985. 168 pages.

This guide is designed to assist host families in understanding the international exchange experience and offers suggestions for helping them become effective host families.

437 Scholarship Research Group. *Scholarships for International Students: A Complete Guide to Colleges and Universities in the United States 1986-88*. Middlebury Heights, Ohio: Scholarship Research Group, 1986. 271 pages.

This reference lists the available scholarship programs, number of awards, and dollar value of awards offered to foreign students in over a thousand colleges and universities.

Immigration Policies

438 Patel, V. R. *A Step-By-Step Guide to Obtaining Green Card from Student Visa*. Dallas, Tex.: Immigration Publications, 1986. 72 pages.

Regulations regarding student immigrant visas are explained. Procedures for attempting to obtain permanent resident status (green cards) for international students who do not wish to leave the United States when their studies are completed are outlined.

439 Smith, Eugene H., and Baron, Marvin J. *Faculty Member's Guide to U.S. Immigration Law*. Washington, D.C.: National Association for Foreign Student Affairs, 1986. 47 pages.

This pamphlet provides a brief summary of immigration laws and regulations affecting students and scholars. It explains the status of the green card and of the F-1, M-1, and J-1 visas.

Foreign Teaching Assistants

440 Althen, Gary. *Manual for Foreign Teaching Assistants*. Iowa City: University of Iowa Office of International Education and Services, 1981. 30 pages.

This brief training manual is designed to accompany an orientation program for foreign teaching assistants and provides an introduction to teaching on an American campus. It contains information and suggestions for foreign teaching assistants, including what is typically expected of them, and discusses the aspects of American higher education that are likely to challenge them.

441 Bailey, Kathleen M.; Pialorski, Frank; and Zukowski/ Faust, Gene (eds.). *Foreign Student Assistants in U.S. Universities.* Washington, D.C.: National Association for Foreign Student Affairs, 1984. 133 pages.

This edited book discusses the problems faced by institutions that employ nonnative English-speaking teaching assistants and the problems faced by these foreign TAs. Various examples of workshops and programs designed to orient and/or train foreign teaching assistants are presented, along with various techniques to evaluate the effectiveness of these programs and of the teaching assistants themselves.

Americans Abroad

442 Anthony, Rebecca, and Roe, Gerald. *Educators' Passport to International Jobs: How to Find and Enjoy Employment Abroad.* Princeton, N.J.: Peterson's Guides, 1984. 181 pages.

This book presents the various aspects of an overseas job search for teaching positions overseas and discusses the types of experiences that overseas teachers report, both in the classroom and in their daily lives.

★443 Council on International Educational Exchange. *The Teenager's Guide to Study, Travel, and Adventure Abroad.* New York: Council on International Educational Exchange, 1987. 280 pages.

This guide discusses types of overseas opportunities available for teenagers and provides guidelines for selecting programs and preparing for international experiences. The second part of the guide lists a large number of programs geared to teenagers and provides relevant information regarding each program.

444 Hess, Gerhard. *Freshmen and Sophomores Abroad: Community Colleges and Overseas Academic Programs.* New York: Teachers College Press, 1982. 194 pages.

In this volume the author presents reasons why American community colleges should develop study abroad programs. It includes information on how to organize and carry out such programs. The problems and possibilities of international exchange programs are discussed and a model, developed at one community college, is presented.

*445 Leerburger, Benedict A. *The Insider's Guide to Foreign Study.* Reading, Mass.: Addison-Wesley, 1987. 579 pages.

This volume contains information about studying and living abroad. American study abroad programs are listed by country and within country by city in which the program is offered.

Cross-Cultural Education

446 Brislin, Richard W. *Cross-Cultural Encounters: Face-to-Face Interaction.* Elmsford, N.Y.: Pergamon Press, 1981. 373 pages.

This book organizes and explains a number of concepts that provide a basis for understanding intergroup interaction. The role of attitudes, thought processes, and reference groups in analyzing and understanding cross-cultural interactions are discussed.

447 Burn, Barbara, B. *Expanding the International Dimension of Higher Education.* San Francisco: Jossey-Bass, 1980. 175 pages.

This report for the Carnegie Council on Policy Studies in Higher Education focuses on the consequences of the lack of knowledge and concern that Americans show toward the international dimensions of their lives.

448 Martin, Judith N. (ed.). "Theories and Methods in Cross-Cultural Orientation." *International Journal of Intercultural Relations,* 1986, *10*(2), 103–258.

This special issue of this journal deals with cross-cultural training and training skills, approaches to cross-cultural orientation, and applications for cross-cultural orientation.

449 Neff, Charles B. (ed.). *Cross-Cultural Learning.* New Directions for Experiential Learning, no. 11. San Francisco: Jossey-Bass, 1981. 88 pages.

This sourcebook provides an examination of experiential learning in different cultures, whether in the United States or abroad. It utilizes case examples to demonstrate ways to improve student services in this area.

450 Pedersen, Paul D. *A Handbook for Developing Multicultural Awareness.* Alexandria, Va.: American Association for Counseling and Development, 1988. 228 pages.

This practical guide addresses the improvement of awareness and communication between culturally diverse individuals. Multicultural development stages, simulation exercises, and other specific techniques are featured, as well as a discussion of multicultural identity and an emphasis on overcoming cultural stereotypes.

Higher Education Internationally

451 Altbach, Philip G. *Higher Education in the Third World: Themes and Variations.* New York: Maruzen, 1982. 228 pages.

This book discusses issues and problems faced by higher education systems and institutions in the Third World that relate to the students and faculty in postsecondary education institutions. Particular emphasis is placed upon the problems and issues faced by Third World universities.

452 Cameron, John, and Hurst, Paul (eds.). *International Handbook of Educational Systems: Sub-Saharan Africa and North Africa and the Middle East.* Vol. 2. Chichester, England: Wiley, 1983. 896 pages.

For a description of this work see entry no. 454.

★453 Clark, Burton R. (ed.). *The School and the University: An International Perspective.* Berkeley: University of California Press, 1985. 337 pages.

This book summarizes secondary and higher education in various countries of the world, including a number of European, Latin American, African, and Asian countries, including Japan and China. It describes the influences and forces that affect the systems of secondary and higher education in each country or area, particularly those affecting the articulation between the two systems.

454 Cowen, Robert, and McLean, Martin (eds.). *International Handbook of Educational Systems. Asia, Australia, and Latin America.* Vol. 3. Chichester, England: Wiley, 1984. 884 pages.

These chapters in each of these handbooks (see also no. 452 and no. 455) cover a wide range of information for each country, including its history, geography, culture, and economy. Additional information is provided regarding the educational system and its development and educational administration and finance.

455 Holmes, Brian (ed.). *International Handbook of Educational Systems: Europe and Canada.* Vol. 1. Chichester, England: Wiley, 1983. 729 pages.

For a description of this work see entry no. 454.

456 Inglis, Christine, and Nash, Rita. *Education in Southeast Asia: A Select Bibliography of English-Language Materials on Education in Indonesia, Malaysia, Philippines, Singapore, and Thailand, 1945–1983.* Brookfield, Vt.: Gower Publishing, 1985. 554 pages.

This volume contains 6,300 listings of books, articles, and reports dealing with Southeast Asian education.

457 Schmida, Leslie C. *Education in the Middle East.* Washington, D.C.: American–Mid East Educational and Training Services, 1983. 143 pages.

This guide presents basic information regarding the educational systems of Middle Eastern countries intended for foreign admissions officers and student placement officers.

Foreign Student Advising Profession

458 Reid, Joy M. (ed.). *Building the Professional Dimension of Educational Exchange.* Yarmouth, Maine: Intercultural Press, 1988. 232 pages.

This compilation of articles is based on papers presented at the 1987 NAFSA Annual Convention. Articles generally deal with the professional development of those in the foreign student advising field.

Periodicals and Annuals

★459 *Academic Year Abroad.* Published annually by the Institute of International Education, 809 United Nations Plaza, New York, N.Y. 10017.

This volume lists and briefly describes over a thousand overseas educational programs sponsored or cosponsored by American colleges and universities, varying in length from an academic quarter to a full academic year or more. Programs are listed by country and include subjects studied, type of institution, highlights of the program, costs, housing, and contact addresses.

460 *Comparative Education Review.* Published four times a year by the Comparative and International Education Society, University of Chicago Press, P.O. Box 37005, Chicago, Ill. 60637.

This periodical publishes articles and book reviews of interest to those in the field of international education. A subscription is included with membership in the Comparative and International Education Society.

461 *International Journal of Intercultural Relations.* Published quarterly by the Society for Intercultural Education, Training, and Research, Pergamon Press, Fairview Park, Elmsford, N.Y. 10523.

The international editorial board research studies carried out in various countries and cultures in the world are published along with abstracts of the articles. The journal is translated into both Spanish and French. Book reviews dealing with intercultural education and relations are included.

★462 *Journal of the Association of International Education Administrators.* Published twice yearly by the Association of International Education Administrators, Washington State University Press, Washington State University, Pullman, Wash. 99164.

The Association of International Education Administrators publishes this journal each spring and fall. It contains articles, reports, and research studies dealing with international education and also reports the meetings and affairs of the association.

★463 *NAFSA Newsletter.* Washington, D.C.: Published eight times a year by the National Association for Foreign Student Affairs, 1860 19th Street NW, Washington, D.C. 20009.

Subscriptions to this approximately thirty-page newsletter are included in the membership fees of the National Association for Foreign Student Affairs. In addition to reporting the business of the association and issues with which the field is concerned, the newsletter also includes announcements of various sources of funding, brief articles on various issues in the field, and announcements of publications, conferences, and international exchanges of interest to foreign student advisers.

464 *Study Abroad.* Biennial publication of the United Nations Educational, Scientific, and Cultural Organization (UNESCO), 7 Place de Fontenoy, 75700, Paris, France.

This biennial publication lists some 3,700 entries describing international study programs in various academic and professional fields along with possibilities of financial assistance. Information is presented on institutions in 124 countries in English, French, or Spanish, according to the official language of correspondence used by UNESCO in that country.

⁊ 10 ⁊

Counseling Centers

Knowledge drawn from psychology has strongly influenced the theory and practice of professionals in many areas of student services, particularly in the field of counseling in student personnel. Research and insights into individual differences, developmental growth, IQ and scholastic aptitude, vocational choice and adjustment, and psychopathology have constituted the knowledge on which counseling is based.

Counselors were the first of the student services staff to become professional in regard to their training, professional organizations, and status. Counselors also remain the most professional of the student services staff, again because of the specific specialized training necessary, their professional organizations with their codes of ethics, and their increasing movement in the direction of accreditation and licensure.

While many of the basic resources in the literature concerned with college counseling are found in various areas of psychology, many others are concerned with the theories and processes of counseling—both individual and group. As there are hundreds, if not thousands, of volumes dealing with various aspects of counseling, no attempt is made within this bibliography to include basic resources in the entire field of counseling. Instead, the focus here is on the organization and functioning of counseling centers on college and university campuses. Persons interested in the various aspects or specialties within the counseling field should refer to the counseling literature for that specific type or aspect of counseling.

Another problem in reviewing the literature regarding counseling on the college campus is that several of the functions of the typical counseling center overlap with the functions of other student services agencies. Some counseling centers have chosen to focus primarily on mental health and personal adjustment counseling and have to a considerable extent yielded the educational and career counseling to other agencies on the campus, such as the career services and placement center. When the role of the college placement office was limited to scheduling interviews and compiling and circulating placement folders, there was little overlap with the function of the counseling center. Now many placement offices have become offices of career services and also provide services that include career counseling, occupational information, and vocational decision-making services. On other campuses much of the mental health counseling may be conducted out of the student health center or referred off campus, with the counseling center's primary role continuing to be that of educational and vocational counseling.

In the past the traditional campus counseling center consisted primarily of counselors in their offices working with individual students who came of their own volition to the counseling center. Counseling centers today are much more likely to be involved in a number of outreach programs. These include programs in the residences, weekend workshops, support groups, career decision-making groups and workshops, and wellness programs. The trend is away from long-term counseling and psychotherapy with individual students toward group and outreach programs designed to reach a much greater number. Counselors are also typically involved in training peer counselors in the residence halls, academic advisers, and orientation leaders.

College staff in counseling centers often continue to work with problems of reading and study skills, but on larger campuses different types of educational skills centers have been established that now specialize in this function. Personal adjustment counseling is ordinarily still an important function of the campus counseling center, but even here, on some campuses, certain types of mental health or psychological services are also offered out of the student health agency on the campus. Due to this, certain important resources in the area of college counseling are also important resources for student services professionals in other agencies. Thus certain references that deal both with counseling and another student service may be found either in this chapter or in another chapter that deals with an overlapping student services function. For example, almost all the resources dealing with career counseling are found in the chapter on career services (Chapter Twelve).

The resources listed here deal first with the administration of counseling centers and then with various issues and policies concerned with college student counseling. In the next section resources describing counseling strategies to deal with different types of problems are included. The last two sections (except for the periodicals) include literature on counseling in community colleges and with the counseling of special populations in higher education.

Administration of Counseling Centers

465 Eyeiwai, Stanley I.; Churchill, William D.; and Cummings, Lawrence T. "The Physical Characteristics of College and University Counseling Services." *Journal of College Student Personnel,* 1983, *24,* 55–60.

This article summarizes the results of a survey of the physical characteristics of counseling center facilities in 134 institutions across the country with a student body of at least 5,000.

★466 Gallagher, Phillip J., and Demos, George D. *Handbook of Counseling in Higher Education.* New York: Praeger, 1983. 331 pages.

This book describes the functions of a psychological counseling center on college and university campuses. The chapters deal with the various roles of counseling center staff and the types of assistance they provide, issues and evaluation problems, psychological assessment services, the use of the *Diagnostic and Statistic Manual of Mental Disorders* (DSM III), ethics and confidentiality, and aspects of counseling center administration. There is an additional chapter that deals with academic advising and career counseling and placement.

467 Giddan, Norman S., and Austin, Michael J. (eds.). *Peer Counseling and Self-Help Groups on Campus.* Springfield, Ill.: Thomas, 1982. 188 pages.

This edited book with nineteen contributors presents an overview of peer counseling programs with a number of examples, particularly from Florida State University. The selection, training, and use of volunteer paraprofessionals are included in the various topics presented.

468 Lewing, Reece L., Jr., and Cowger, Ernest L., Jr. "Time Spent on College Counselor Functions." *Journal of College Student Personnel,* 1982, *23,* 41–48.

This study of counselors in counseling centers at institutions of varying sizes reports how much time they spent in performing nine different counselor functions. Variations among these functions across institutions of varying sizes are reported.

469 Owens, Hilda F.; Witten, Charles H.; and Bailey, Walter R. (eds.). *College Student Personnel Administration: An Anthology.* Springfield, Ill.: Thomas, 1982. 391 pages.

For a description of this work see entry no. 26.

470 Schneider, Lynette D. "Counseling." In William T. Packwood, (ed.), *College Student Personnel Services.* Springfield, Ill.: Thomas, 1977, pp. 340–367.

This chapter reviews literature related to the organization, functions, and programs of college counseling centers. Literature related to administration, financing, and counseling services personnel is also summarized. For a description of Packwood's complete work see entry no. 27.

471 Schoenberg, B. Mark (ed). *A Handbook and Guide for College and University Counseling Centers.* Westport, Conn.: Greenwood Press, 1978. 305 pages.

This book is a collection of articles, many by directors or former directors of counseling centers, containing information about the organization and management of these centers, and a discussion of issues often faced in such agencies. In addition, there are chapters covering ethical considerations, education and training roles of the center, the use of case conferences, and issues in consultation and referral.

472 Talley, Joseph E., and Rockwell, W. J. Kenneth (eds.). *Counseling and Psychotherapy Services for University Students.* Springfield, Ill.: Thomas, 1985. 109 pages.

The chapters in this edited volume deal with the various professional services offered by most college counseling centers. Several deal with the needs of students and the types of psychological services provided. Emergency and intake procedures are described, along with the roles of different types of mental health personnel and consultation and communication procedures.

473 Tryon, Georgiana S. "A Review of the Literature Concerning Perceptions of and Preferences for Counseling Center Services." *Journal of College Student Personnel,* 1980, *21,* 304–311.

This article reviews studies over a twenty-five-year period dealing with student concerns and student perceptions of counseling centers and where students turn for help with various problems.

474 Walz, Garry R., and Bleuer, Jeanne C. (eds.). *Counseling Software Guide.* Alexandria, Va.: American Association for Counseling and Development, 1989. 491 pages.

This guide contains descriptions of 526 computer programs of interest to counselors. In addition to the software descriptions, trends and developments in counseling software are discussed, and a number of critical reviews are included regarding software for particular purposes in counseling. Other resources included in the volume are an evaluation checklist, computer capability information, and publisher addresses.

475 Whiteley, Scott M.; Mahaffey, Patrick J.; and Geer, Carol A. "The Campus Counseling Center: A Profile of Staffing Patterns and Services." *Journal of College Student Personnel,* 1987. *28,* 71–81.

This article reports the results of a study of almost a thousand institutions dealing with the characteristics of counseling center staff and the functions of these centers.

Issues and Policies

★476 American Association for Counseling and Development. *Foundations for Policy in Guidance and Counseling.* Alexandria, Va.: American Association for Counseling and Development, 1982. 221 pages.

A comprehensive reference for future policy decisions, this book examines past and present policies upon which guidance and counseling programs have been structured. It addresses the many issues that affect the work of the counselor and is a comprehensive reference for future policy decisions.

★477 Biggs, Donald A., and Blocher, Donald H. *Foundations of Ethical Counseling.* New York: Springer, 1987. 192 pages.

This book explores the philosophical and cognitive bases of ethical counseling. Case examples and ethical dilemmas from counseling practice are included.

478 Gross, Bruce H., and Weinberger, Linda E. (eds.). *The Mental Health Professional and the Legal System.* New Directions for Mental Health Services, no. 16. San Francisco: Jossey-Bass, 1982. 105 pages.

This sourcebook examines the issues regarding the legal use of psychiatric data and information. Specific guidelines are offered for the mental health professional whose advice may be sought by members of a judicial system for decision-making purposes.

479   Hopkins, Bruce R., and Anderson, Barbara S. *The Counselor and the Law.* (2nd ed.) Alexandria, Va.: American Association for Counseling and Development, 1985. 141 pages.

This book describes the legal aspects of confidentiality and privileged communications within the counselor-client relationship, both civil and criminal liability including malpractice, breach of contract, and contributing to the delinquency of a minor. Legal aspects of private practice and professional liability insurance are discussed.

480   Rayman, Jack R., and Garis, Jeffrey W. "Counseling." In M. Lee Upcraft, John N. Gardner, and Associates, *The Freshman Year Experience: Helping Students Survive and Succeed in College.* San Francisco: Jossey-Bass, 1989, pp. 129–141.

This chapter discusses various issues involved in the counseling of freshmen. The authors present seven general recommendations regarding the types and functions of counseling services that should be provided to freshmen students. Emphasis is on outreach services to meet the needs of freshmen. For a description of Upcraft and Garner's complete work see entry no. 100.

Counseling Strategies

481   Altmaier, Elizabeth M. (ed.). *Helping Students Manage Stress.* New Directions in Student Services, no. 21. San Francisco: Jossey-Bass, 1983. 108 pages.

This overview of the theory and research on stress provides a valuable resource to the student services professional attempting to understand and assess the impact of stress on students. Programs addressing individuals and campus-wide strategies are included.

482 Anderson, Wayne P. *Innovative Counseling: A Handbook of Readings.* Alexandria, Va.: American Association for Counseling and Development, 1986. 225 pages.

This handbook, a collection of articles from the *Journal of Counseling and Development,* features problem-solving information directed toward practicing counselors who may not have specific training in a particular area. Designed as a reference tool, it includes information on sleep or eating disorders, homosexuality, aging issues, and burnout.

483 Barrow, John C. *Fostering Cognitive Development of Students: A New Approach to Counseling and Program Planning.* San Francisco: Jossey-Bass 1986. 380 pages.

For a description of this work see entry no. 60.

484 Conyne, Robert K. "Toward Primary Prevention: An Evaluation Research Approach for College Counselors." *Journal of College Student Personnel,* 1980, *21,* 426–430.

This article presents various arguments for the importance of primary prevention programs among the functions of college counselors. It describes a research-dissemination-utilization approach to the development of such programs.

★485 Gysbers, Norman C., and Associates. *Designing Careers: Counseling to Enhance Education, Work, and Leisure.* San Francisco: Jossey-Bass, 1984. 660 pages.

This book, containing chapters by a number of noted authorities in the field, considers the psychological, sociologial, and economic perspectives influencing career and lifestyle decisions. Produced by the National Vocational Guidance Association, chapters in the book discuss the changing meanings given to career development, the changing structure of occupations, new theories and techniques of career development, and projected responses to future changes and trends.

486 Hanfmann, Eugenia. *Effective Therapy for College Students: Alternatives to Traditional Counseling.* San Francisco: Jossey-Bass, 1978. 347 pages.

In this book the author presents a model of time-limited individual verbal psychotherapy designed to promote significant positive change in a variety of the typical problems faced by college students. It includes practical suggestions for organizing counseling services that will meet the needs of large numbers of college students while staying within reasonable budgetary considerations.

487 Kapes, Jerome T., and Mastie, Marjorie M. (eds.). *A Counselor's Guide to Career Assessment Instruments.* (2nd ed.) Alexandria, Va.: American Association for Counseling and Development, 1988. 351 pages.

For a description of this work see entry No. 577.

488 May, Robert (ed.). *Psychoanalytic Psychotherapy in a College Context.* New York: Praeger, 1988. 196 pages.

In the early chapters in this volume the use of psychoanalytic therapy in college counseling centers is described, along with the issues and constraints that accompany its use. The later chapters deal with the use of this psychotherapeutic technique with particular types of student problems and include accompanying case examples.

489 Muñoz, Rodrigo A. (ed.). *Treating Anxiety Disorders.* New Directions for Mental Health Services, no. 32. San Francisco: Jossey-Bass, 1986. 115 pages.

This volume provides comprehensive information on a variety of anxiety disorders and effective diagnosis and treatment. Client vignettes are presented, as well as a discussion of the incidence and prevalence of these disorders. Also featured are the influence of heredity and environment on vulnerability to the disorders and a discussion of factors leading to their development and control.

490 Shelton, John I. *Behavior Modification for Counseling Centers: A Guide to Program Development.* Washington, D.C.: American College Personnel Association, 1976. 184 pages.

This presentation of various types of behavior modification programs used on college campuses includes descriptions of specific programs and references relevant to the particular types of behavior modification techniques. Types of programs range from assertiveness training through weight control, social skills training, roommate conflicts, and biofeedback.

491 Talley, Joseph E., and Rockwell, W. J. Kenneth (eds.). *Counseling and Psychotherapy with College Students.* New York: Praeger, 1986. 187 pages.

This book briefly describes individual counseling techniques useful in college counseling centers. These approaches are applied to several types of psychological problems often faced by students.

492 Whitman, Neal A.; Spendlove, David C.; and Clark, Claire H. (eds.). *Student Stress: Effects and Solutions.* Washington, D.C.: Association for the Study of Higher Education, 1984. 106 pages.

This publication reviews research studies that have been concerned with the sources and effects of stress among students and summarizes individual and institutional attempts to deal with such concerns. A comprehensive reference list dealing with the topic is included.

Counseling in Community Colleges

493 Amada, Gerald (ed.). *Mental Health on the Community College Campus.* (2nd ed.) Lanham, Md.: University Press of America, 1985. 139 pages.

This compilation of articles addresses the administration and delivery of mental health programs for a seldom researched population—the community college student. This book addresses concerns of both the professional and the student.

494 Paradise, Louis V., and Long, Thomas J. *Counseling in the Community College: Models and Approaches.* New York: Praeger, 1981. 220 pages.

This book discusses counseling in the community college with particular emphasis upon the context for the counseling, which includes the commitment to the local community and the egalitarian commitment of the community college with its different mission and heterogeneous student population. The problem-solving model that includes both behavioral and rational approaches in both individual and group sessions is emphasized. Organization and roles of the counseling center and of the entire student affairs program for a community college are also included.

495 Thurston, Alice S., and Robbins, William A. (eds.). *Counseling: A Crucial Function for the 1980s.* New Directions for Community Colleges, no. 43, San Francisco: Jossey-Bass, 1983. 137 pages.

This innovative look at counseling services for community colleges considers the specific issues that community colleges and their students must face, including the need for their counseling professionals to sometimes fill multiple roles on campus.

Counseling Special Populations

496 Agras, W. Stewart. *Eating Disorders: Management of Obesity, Bulimia, and Anorexia Nervosa.* Elmsford, N.Y.: Pergamon Press, 1987. 144 pages.

This volume presents treatment methods for the management of obesity, bulimia, and anorexia nervosa, disorders in which the patients' primary concern is with weight and body image. Assessment techniques and detailed treatment programs for these disorders are outlined.

497 Gelatt, H. B.; Schlossberg, Nancy K.; Herr, Edwin L.; Lynch, Ann Q.; Chickering, Arthur W.; Walz, Garry R.; and Benjamin, Libby. *New Perspectives on Counseling Adult Learners.* Ann Arbor, Mich.: ERIC/CAPS Publications, 1984. 87 pages.

This edited monograph with papers by several well-known writers in the fields of counseling and adult education is designed to provide new ideas and information useful in the counseling of adult learners.

498 Larocca, Felix E. F. (ed.). *Eating Disorders.* New Directions for Mental Health Services, no. 31. San Francisco: Jossey-Bass, 1986. 127 pages.

This volume provides comprehensive information on a variety of eating disorders, including anorexia, bulimia, and several lesser-known disorders. The variety of treatment alternatives are reviewed, including consideration of tubefeeding and patients' opinion of it. The connection between eating disorders and mood disorders is also investigated.

★499 Neuman, Patricia A., and Halvorson, Patricia A. *Anorexia Nervosa and Bulimia: A Handbook for Counselors and Therapists.* New York: Van Nostrand Reinhold, 1983. 272 pages.

This book provides a review of the literature relating to research and treatment for both anorexia and bulimia. It provides examples of diagnostic criteria, therapeutic goals and focus, and various therapeutic techniques. Also discussed is the extreme difficulty in the treatment of such eating disorders currently found too often on many college campuses.

500 Scher, Murray; Stevens, Mark; Good, Glen; and Eichenfield, Greg (eds.). *Handbook of Counseling and Psychotherapy with Men.* Newbury Park, Calif.: Sage, 1987. 400 pages.

This volume contains twenty-five chapters by different authors dealing with techniques and concerns in counseling men and the developmental issues in men's lives. Additional chapters deal with counseling men from different special populations and ethnic groups.

Periodicals and Annuals

★501 *Counseling Psychologist.* Published quarterly by the Division of Counseling Psychology of the American Psychological Association, 1200 17th Street NW, Washington, D.C. 20036.

Each issue centers on a theme or issue in the field and contains several other articles and a section dealing with the activities of the Division of Counseling Psychology. A subscription is included with division membership.

★502 *Directory of Counseling Services.* Published by the International Association of Counseling Services, 5999 Stevenson Avenue, Alexandria, Va. 22304.

This directory lists those counseling services in colleges, universities, and public and private agencies that meet the standards for accreditation by the International Association of Counseling Services. Names, addresses, types of counseling, fees, and other information are included for each counseling organization. The Directory is in a loose-leaf format and updated packets are provided annually.

★503 *Journal of Counseling and Development* (formerly *Personnel and Guidance Journal*). Ten issues a year, published by the American Association for Counseling and Development, 5999 Stevenson Avenue, Alexandria, Va. 22304.

This journal includes articles on issues, theory, and research in counseling and student development. A subscription is included with membership in the American Association for Counseling and Development.

★504 *Journal of Counseling Psychology.* Six issues per year. Published by the American Psychological Association, Mt. Royal and Guilford Avenues, Baltimore, Md. 21202.

This journal publishes articles, primarily research based, of interest to psychologists and counselors who work in a wide variety of agencies and settings.

505 *Journal of Multicultural Counseling and Development.* Published four times a year by the Association for Multicultural Counseling and Development of the American Association for Counseling and Development, 5999 Stevenson Avenue Alexandria, Va. 22304.

This journal contains articles on research, theory, and program applications dealing with multicultural and ethnic cultural minorities in all areas of counseling and development. It includes articles dealing with minority interests and experiences.

✐ 11 ✑

Student Activities
and College Unions

Although student activities—which include large numbers of student organizations, extracurricular activities, student government, and many important out-of-class programs—exist on virtually all campuses, there is not a great deal of literature dealing with this subject. On the one hand, many in higher education view these types of out-of-class activities, in which many student affairs professionals typically spend large amounts of energy and resources, as strictly the "sideshow." In contrast to this, there are large numbers of students and alumni who feel that for them, far greater learning took place through their involvement in such activities than through the structured experiences in the classrooms, laboratories, and libraries. In addition, many of the student groups and activities play an important role in the public relations and marketing of the institution and, therefore, become important factors in the very livelihood of the institution.

Staff members having responsibilities for student activities on the campus have always been interested in attempting to teach such skills as effective programming techniques, methods of managing effective organizations, and leadership skills. More recently many have also been given the responsibility of designing educational programming on the campus dealing with such issues as sexual harassment, alcohol education, AIDS, and substance abuse. Those institutions that attempt to teach moral and ethical values have been concerned that campus activities also reflect these values. Student political organizations and the campus press also typically come under the auspices of student activities staff, and during the era of student activism in the 1960s a great deal of staff energy was consumed dealing with such organizations and issues.

During the 1960s court decisions greatly restricted the amount of control, both regulatory and financial, that student activities offices possessed in regard to student activities, student government, and the campus press. More recent court decisions regarding the legal liability of institutions and campus organizations have also had an impact. References to literature related to such legal aspects are found in this chapter and also in Chapter Four.

On most campuses responsibility for student activities is shared with such other student services as residence life and the campus union. On some campuses the majority of student activities originate from one of these two services. Responsibilities for departmental and other special interest clubs, intramural sports and athletics, and foreign student organizations may also be found in other departments on the campus rather than in the office of student activities. Fraternities and sororities may have their major campus connections with the student activities office, although on some campuses these organizations are supervised by residence life staff. In this volume fraternities and sororities are considered as a part of student activities, and relevant literature is placed in this chapter following those listings that deal with program development and other student organizations.

Related to the area of student activities, usually by location and often through shared staff members, is college union administration. Unions are often integral parts of the nonclassroom experience for many students. Typically, they house many of the student activities, student group offices, and a variety of other student services from food services to bookstores, craft centers, and art galleries.

The student services professionals who work within the context of a union setting are usually involved in more business operations than some of the other services on campus. Besides food services and the overall building services and operations, union professionals are also often involved in providing hotel and convention or conference facilities for nonstudents.

Operating and maintaining a facility that is often one of the largest and most intensively utilized buildings on the campus with a variety of operations requires much energy and administrative skill. At times these aspects overshadow the educational programming and student development functions of the union. This is especially true on campuses where the union must break even or show a substantial profit. On the other hand, if the business operations are losing money, then there is likely to be no funding left for programming and student activities, and indeed these functions are often only possible with the profits that come from the business operations.

The literature on the union setting reflects the emphasis of the work done in the field. The Association of College Unions-International (ACU-I) has provided a sharp focus for this aspect of the profession, publishing numerous texts, handbooks, and periodicals to address the specific concerns of union management. In fact, almost the entire body of literature for this area can be traced directly to ACU-I.

In contrast to this central organization that supports much practitioner-based literature, in the field of student activities the National Association of Campus Activities has been less active, and consequently the literature is more sporadic. Since the field of student activities has lacked a journal that deals specifically with student activities and organizations, the primary source of periodical literature in this area is found in the generalist student services journals. Large numbers of journal articles dealing with student activities are not found in the literature, but the majority that have appeared have been published in the *NASPA Journal* (no. 3), the *Journal of College Student Development* (no. 1), and *Initiatives* (no. 2). This lack of resources in the literature can also be tied to the nature of student activities work, which requires much energy and resources on the part of the professional. Student activities tend to attract younger members of the profession and due to the considerable energy and time necessary for student activities, there is often a high burnout rate. Therefore, there is a tendency either to leave the field of student affairs entirely or to move on to other administrative posts or other people-oriented occupations. Furthermore, these positions frequently are entry-level positions, often open to persons who have not had training in student development. Consequently, with little extra time and often minimal training in student development, there is little impetus to invest time in research and professional publications.

The highly centralized practitioner-oriented specialty area of union management, in combination with the rather unorganized and demanding area of student activities, yields a rather meager body of literature geared toward specific, practitioner-oriented topics within each specialized area and few theoretical or philosophical articles. As these fields continue to become more specialized, this trend will undoubtedly continue, but a more extensive range of practical information will become available.

Program Development

506 Barr, Margaret J., and Keating, Lou Ann (eds.). *Establishing Effective Programs.* New Directions for Student Services, no. 7. San Francisco: Jossey-Bass, 1979. 106 pages.

This sourcebook is a comprehensive guide for determining need and resources before planning programs. Also discussed are how to change existing programs to respond to changing conditions or new ideas and how to train staff for optimal program delivery.

507 Brown, Robert D., and DeCoster, David A. (eds.). *Mentoring-Transcript Systems for Promoting Student Growth.* New Directions in Student Services, no. 19. San Francisco: Jossey-Bass, 1982. 116 pages.

This sourcebook provides an explanation of a system that documents students' growth that is not adequately reflected in traditional transcripts. Members of the faculty or student services professionals serve as mentors to students and advise them in a broad range of areas.

508 Dean, James C., and Bryan, William A. (eds.). *Alcohol Programming for Higher Education.* Alexandria, Va.: American College Personnel Association, 1982. 144 pages.

This brief volume attempts to present a systematic approach to providing an effective program to deal with alcohol-related problems on the campus. The program is designed for a total campus community and focuses not only on students but also on employee assistance programs for staff and faculty.

509 Goodale, Thomas G. (ed.). *Alcohol and the College Student.* New Directions in Student Services, no. 35. San Francisco: Jossey-Bass, 1986. 68 pages.

This sourcebook addresses the legal, educational, and health problems that result from alcohol use on campus. It evaluates current programs such as Students Against Drunk Drivers and provides guidelines and reports on legal liability of colleges for student drinking.

510 Leafgren, Fred (ed.). *Developing Campus Recreation and Wellness Programs.* New Directions for Student Services, no. 34. San Francisco: Jossey-Bass, 1986. 95 pages.

This volume provides a valuable resource for implementing a complete student recreation and wellness program, including financial issues, building construction, and general maintenance strategies.

511 Roberts, Dennis C. (eds.). *Student Leadership Programs for Higher Education.* Alexandria, Va.: American College Personnel Association Media, 1981. 239 pages.

This book provides a number of different models and programs for promoting the development of leadership among college students in several different types of student activities and in a number of different types of student populations and subcultures. Included are chapters providing information about specific programs and resources that can be drawn upon in the development and delivery of such programs.

Program Evaluation

512 Baugher, Dan (ed.). *Measuring Effectiveness.* New Directions for Program Evaluation, no. 11. San Francisco: Jossey-Bass, 1981. 112 pages.

This sourcebook comprehensively explores problems and possible solutions in measuring organizational effectiveness of academic and educational systems and programs.

513 Chamberlain, Philip C. *Student Activities Assessment Model (SAAM).* Bloomington, Ind.: Association of College Unions-International, 1987. 59 pages.

The book presents a comprehensive framework for unions to adopt for the purpose of assessing their alignment with the standards adopted by the Council for the Advancement of Standards for Student Services Development Programs. This model is designed to assist campuses in determining how effectively their activities programs are meeting their goals and the needs of the constituent groups.

514 Hanson, Gary R. (ed.). *Evaluating Program Effectiveness.* New Directions for Student Services, no. 1. San Francisco: Jossey-Bass, 1978. 104 pages.

This inaugural issue of New Directions for Student Services sets the tone for the series by addressing the elements of evaluation theory and offering practical advice about the evaluation process, including characteristics of the evaluator as consultant.

515 Sechrest, Lee (ed.). *Training Program Evaluators.* New Directions for Program Evaluation, no. 8. San Francisco: Jossey-Bass, 1980. 94 pages.

This sourcebook outlines professional training requirements including research design and analysis, problem solving, and how to acquire the basic skills necessary to serve clients.

Group. Development

516 Goodstein, Leonard D., and Pfeiffer, J. William (eds.).
The Annual Series for Facilitators, Trainers, and Consultants.
San Diego, Calif.: University Associates.

These volumes have been published annually since 1972 by
several editors from University Associates. They include descriptions of structured experiences, inventories, and questionnaires
for use in group processes or in evaluation, group resource
materials, and outlines, discussions, and lectures for group
leaders.

★517 Pfeiffer, J. William, and Jones, John E. *A Handbook of
Structured Experiences for Human Relations Training.* 9 vols.
San Diego, Calif.: University Associates, 1973–1982.

These nine volumes of structured experiences focus on individual
behavior, constructive feedback, processing, and psychological
integration within a group setting. Readers are free to duplicate
the forms, activities, and instruments for their own use.

★518 Winston, Roger B., Jr.; Bonney, Warren C.; Miller,
Theodore K.; and Dagley, John C. *Promoting Student
Development Through Intentionally Structured Groups: Principles,
Techniques, and Applications.* San Francisco: Jossey-Bass,
1988. 408 pages.

Student affairs professionals advise and organize many different
types of student groups, and this volume will assist them in applying the knowledge of group theory and group dynamics in
their work with these groups. Included are the stages of group
development, evaluating the group's effectiveness, development
of effective group leadership, and a sample group leader's manual
for guiding structured groups.

Student Organizations

519 Caruso, Robert, and Travelstead, Will W. (eds.). *Enhancing Campus Judicial Systems.* New Directions for Student Services, no. 39. San Francisco: Jossey-Bass, 1987. 102 pages.

This comprehensive description of planning and management issues for campus judicial programs considers administration of these programs and services in light of recent court decisions and federal regulations.

520 Downey, Ronald G.; Bosco, Pat J.; and Silver, Edward M. "Long-Term Outcomes of Participation in Student Government." *Journal of College Student Personnel,* 1984, *25,* 245–250.

This article reports on a follow-up study of students who had been elected to student government positions matched with a comparable group without such participation. Those involved in student government activities reported greater satisfaction with their lives on the campus but no long-term or short-term outcomes, either positive or negative, in their postcollege lives were found to be associated with involvement in college student government.

521 Gibbs, Annette. "Mandatory Student Activity Fees: Educational and Legal Considerations." *Journal of College Student Personnel,* 1980, *21,* 535–540.

This article examines some of the legal questions institutions have faced in the courts regarding the constitutionality of mandatory student activity fees. Policies are suggested regarding the collection and expenditure of student activity fees.

522 Miller, Theodore K., and Jones, John D. "Out-of-Class Activities." In Arthur W. Chickering and Associates, *The Modern American College: Responding to the New Realities of Diverse Students and a Changing Society.* San Francisco: Jossey-Bass, 1981, pp. 657–671.

The authors identify ways in which institutions can become responsive to various student needs by sponsoring out-of-class activities. They describe benefits to student independence, social relationships, career planning, education for leadership, and recreation. The emphasis is on the ways in which out-of-class activities can contribute to total student development. For a description of Chickering's complete work see entry no. 85.

523 Schmidt, Marlin R., and Blaska, Betty. "Student Activities." In William T. Packwood (ed.), *College Student Personnel Services.* Springfield, Ill.: Thomas, 1977, pp. 153–178.

In this chapter the authors review literature concerned with organized student activities on the college campus through 1975. The broad functions of student activities are discussed and the literature reviewed includes that concerned with fraternities and sororities, student government, and political and religious groups. For a description of Packwood's complete work see entry no. 27.

★524 Schuh, John H. (ed.). *A Handbook for Student Group Advisers.* Alexandria, Va.: American College Personnel Association, 1986. 202 pages.

This volume contains chapters by a group of student affairs practitioners with wide experience advising student groups. It provides a rationale, advice, usable ideas, and recommended resources for the types of work, problems, and questions typically faced by advisers of student groups and organizations.

Fraternities and Sororities

★525 Bryan, William A., and Schwartz, Robert A. (eds.). *The Eighties: Challenges for Fraternities and Sororities.* Alexandria, Va.: American College Personnel Association, 1983. 170 pages.

This volume contains thirteen selections by different authors who discuss the current and future challenges faced by fraternities and sororities. It also reviews available research, approaches to evaluating fraternity and sorority life, and management, legal, and minority issues faced by these groups.

526 Keller, Michael J., and Hart, Derrell. "The Effects of Sorority and Fraternity Rush on Students' Self-Images." *Journal of College Student Personnel,* 1982, *23,* 257–261.

This article reports on a study of the students who participated in sorority and fraternity rush at a midwestern university, focusing on the consequences of rush for students who were accepted and not accepted by such membership. Neutral to positive self-assessments were reported by those who pledged, while those who did not pledge reported negative self-assessments.

527 Marlowe, Ann F., and Auvenshine, C. Dwight. "Greek Membership: Its Impact on the Moral Development of College Freshmen." *Journal of College Student Personnel,* 1982, *23,* 53–57.

This influence of fraternity or sorority affiliation on Kohlbergian moral development was explored. No significant relationship to Greek membership was found for this type of development.

528 Winston, Roger B., Jr.; Nettles, William R., III; and Opper, John H., Jr. (eds.). *Fraternities and Sororities on the Contemporary College Campus.* New Directions for Student Services, no. 40. San Francisco: Jossey-Bass, 1987. 123 pages.

This volume addresses topics such as hazing, substance abuse, acquaintance/date rape, and racial prejudice. It offers administrators and other student services professionals practical suggestions for dealing with such problems within the Greek system.

Student Press

529 Ingelhart, Louis E. *Freedom for the College Student Press: Court Cases and Related Decisions Defining the Campus Fourth Estate Boundaries.* Westport, Conn.: Greenwood Press, 1985. 229 pages.

This book examines the constitutional guarantees of free press, particularly as they relate to student publications in public and private higher education institutions. It also contains chapters dealing with such aspects of student publications as liability, obscenity, funding, libel, and copyrights.

530 Schuh, John H. (ed.). *Enhancing Relationships with the Student Press.* New Directions in Student Services, no. 33. San Francisco: Jossey-Bass, 1986. 95 pages.

This sourcebook is an overall guide for working with the student press, from advising student journalists, to ways of dealing with campus controversies and other public relations problems, to the legal framework within which the student press must operate. This volume also addresses how the mission of the student press fits with the overall institutional mission.

College Unions

Overview

531 Butts, Porter. *State of the College Union Around the World.* Ithaca, N.Y.: Cornell University, 1967. 342 pages.

This book offers an overview of the types of unions around the world and the services they provide, including a directory of the buildings in countries other than the United States. Although this book was published over twenty years ago, it represents a "classic" in this specialty area and should be considered for a thorough understanding of the field.

532 Butts, Porter. *The College Union Idea.* Ithaca, N.Y.: Cornell University, 1971. 148 pages.

This compilation of writings and addresses by Porter Butts covers the beginnings of the college union movement from early debating societies and men's clubs through each decade of today's unions from the 1920s through the 1960s. This publication outlines the major forces shaping the college union and the major changes evident over its development.

533 *College Unions: Fifty Facts.* Bloomington, Ind.: Association of College Unions-International, 1986. 12 pages.

This pamphlet provides "a concise collection of information about the development, history, purposes, programs, and financing of college unions."

534 Davis, Nancy T. (ed.). *Annotated Bibliography of the College Union.* Vol. 4. College Unions at Work Series, no. 7. Bloomington, Ind.: Association of College Unions-International, 1984. 155 pages.

This bibliography provides summaries of articles published between 1978 and 1983 that pertain to student unions and student activities. (Volumes 1 to 3, covering articles published between 1915 and 1977, are also available from ACU-I.)

535 Klepper, William M. (ed.). *The Impact of College Unions and Their Programs on Today's Students.* College Unions at Work Series, no. 9. Bloomington, Ind.: Association of College Unions-International, 1981. 64 pages.

With contributions by Arthur Chickering, Gary R. Hanson, Ernest Kovacs, and W. Max Wise, this volume provides guidelines for union professionals facing the changes in colleges and universities.

536 Packwood, William T. "Union." In William T. Packwood (ed.), *College Student Personnel Services,* Springfield,
Ill.: Thomas, 1977, pp. 179–205.

Literature related to student unions is reviewed in this chapter.
Topics covered include functions and purposes of unions, administration and staffing, programming, food service, and cultural affairs. The chapter concludes with an extensive list of
references. For a description of Packwood's complete work see
entry no. 27.

Administration

537 Brattain, William Edwin. *The Administration of College
Union and Campus Activities.* Bloomington, Ind.: T.I.S.
Publications, 1981. 319 pages.

This textbook in the administration of college unions and campus activities provides a comprehensive overview of the history
and development of college unions, the role of unions in the
university setting, and the management of unions including
planning, professional organization, programming, public relations, and food service. A discussion of contributors to the college union movement is also presented.

538 Chamberlain, Philip C. *A Problem-Solving Casebook for College Unions.* Bloomington, Ind.: Association of College
Unions-International, 1981. 136 pages.

This book features cases developed from real problems as indicated on a survey of college union workers. Problem solving
is considered in the context of decision making, with the process itself being highlighted. Examples of cases presented include alcohol policy, program and space conflicts, equipment
use, guest speakers, and security.

539 Geltner, Frank J. *Acuition I.* Bloomington, Ind.: Association of College Unions-International, 1985. 72 pages.

This publication provides a comprehensive examination of the state of computer applications in the student union and student activities field. The topics included range from a discussion of applications and implementation procedures to a list of contact persons.

540 Geltner, Frank J. *Acuition II.* Bloomington, Ind.: Association of College Unions-International, 1987. 30 pages.

This publication presents results from a 1985–86 computer use survey, providing information on computer use in food service and room scheduling, graphics, system selection, and computer obsolescence.

541 Jenkins, Jack, and McQueen, Sidney. *Administration and Operation of the College Union.* College Unions at Work Series, no. 1. Bloomington, Ind.: Association of College Unions-International, 1973. 319 pages.

A survey of 278 colleges and universities yielded the data for this study, which examines administrative and operational patterns of college unions over the previous twenty years.

542 Plakidas, Shirley. *Standards for Professional Staff Preparation in College Unions and Student Activities.* Bloomington, Ind.: Association of College Unions-International, 1986. 13 pages.

This revision of standards covers goals of college unions and provides guidelines for professional positions within the field.

Planning

543 Butts, Porter. *Planning College Union Facilities for Multiple Uses.* Bloomington, Ind.: Association of College Unions-International, 1966. 112 pages.

This book presents an overview of planning strategies to maximize the efficient use of available space, including graphic presentations. Although outdated, it was written by one of the pioneers in the field and is still an important resource.

544 Eldred, Linda. *The Program Planner's Workbook: A Creative and Systematic Approach.* Bloomington, Ind.: Association of College Unions-International, 1985. 136 pages.

This workbook provides a comprehensive how-to for every area of program planning. Planning stages are outlined, with recommendations for needs assessment, goal setting, training, committee functions, implementation, and evaluation. Furthermore, a sampler provides additional information regarding physical layout, communication, and resource lists. Useful graphics are included with each planning stage.

545 Noffke, Frank. *Planning for a College Union.* (2nd ed.) College Unions at Work Series, no. 4. Bloomington, Ind.: Association of College Unions-International, 1987. 34 pages.

The planning and construction stages of union development are discussed by a former union director, with an emphasis on demonstrating how effective planning of the building can cut costs.

Programming

546 Hull, Laura. *Lectures Programming.* College Unions at Work Series, no. 10. Bloomington, Ind.: Association of College Unions-International, 1985. 29 pages.

This monograph provides information on developing a lectures program, including funding, scheduling, publicity, special events, and faculty relations. The discussion includes major and limited series as well as a list of speaker agencies.

547 *Regional Conference Manual.* Bloomington, Ind.: Association of College Unions-International, 1985.

The planning and implementation of a regional conference is outlined in this manual. A comprehensive discussion of operations, including publicity, finances, transportation, and housing is presented, as well as information regarding programs and evaluations.

★548 *A Resource Guide to Outdoor Programs.* Bloomington, Ind.: Committee on Outdoor Programs, Association of College Unions-International, 1981. 331 pages.

Survey results of 200 existing collegiate outdoor programs are presented, along with information helpful in developing a successful program, including start-up techniques, four organizational models, information sources, a bibliography, and a national equipment inventory.

549 Temte, Anne, and Feltner, Camille Smith. *The Union Recreation Area.* College Unions at Work Series, no. 5. Bloomington, Ind.: Association of College Unions-International, 1985. 55 pages.

Based on a 1983 recreational study, this monograph examines usage patterns and identifies trends and general philosophies of recreation programs. An extensive bibliography is also included.

550 *Women's Resource/Program Manual.* Bloomington, Ind.: Association of College Unions-International, 1979. 34 pages.

This manual serves as a guide for developing women's programs by providing a description of programs and services currently provided by college unions. It includes lists of resource centers, speakers, women's organizations, and other resources.

★551 Wood, Stayton. *A Resource Manual for Designing Training Programs*. Bloomington, Ind.: Association of College Unions-International, 1981. 336 pages.

This manual considers training programs and includes a model and exercises for the training process within the context of a college union.

Art

552 Howe, Nanci, and Gerhart, George (eds.). *In Search of Art*. Bloomington, Ind.: Association of College Unions-International, 1980. 32 pages.

A guide for planning art exhibits, film programs, and craft programming, this directory also lists vendors, a bibliography, and a roster of professional arts and service organizations.

553 Kasler, Barbara. *Programming for Crafts: A Resources Primer*. College Unions at Work Series, no. 8. Bloomington, Ind.: Association of College Unions-International, 1975. 20 pages.

This primer discusses start-up, planning, financial, and staffing concerns for a union craft center. A list of resources, such as books, periodicals, catalogues, and organizations, is included.

554 Krueger, Patricia Ann. *Art and Everything*. College Unions at Work Series, no. 3. Bloomington, Ind.: Association of College Unions-International, 1972. 25 pages.

Information regarding the administration of art exhibits is provided, including alarm system diagrams, sample exhibits, and booking contracts.

Periodicals and Annuals

★**555** *Bulletin.* Published six times a year by the Association of College Unions-International, Central Office, 400 E. Seventh Street, Bloomington, Ind. 47405.

This official journal of the Association of College Unions-International (ACU-I) focuses on trends and policies within student activities and college unions. It provides information regarding program planning, management, and building planning.

556 *Conference Proceedings.* Published annually by the Association of College Unions-International, Central Office, 400 E. Seventh Street, Bloomington, Ind. 47405.

This publication is a compilation of selected papers and keynote addresses from the annual ACU-I conference.

557 *Directory.* Annual publication of the Association of College Unions-International, Central Office, 400 E. Seventh Street, Bloomington, Ind. 47405.

This annual roster of all institutional and individual members of ACU-I also lists the association's officers and committee rosters.

558 *Resource Notebook.* Commission on Educational Programs and Services, Association of College Unions-International, 400 East Seventh Street, Bloomington, Ind. 47405.

This publication was designed to be an on-going, informal notebook, to provide members with specific usable information and resources. Presented in a how-to format, the notebook includes such topics as the physical building, organization, programming, services and amenities, and student activities. Approximately 12 articles written by members were added to the notebook on a quarterly basis. The notebook was begun in 1980 and publication was terminated in 1985. It is now available on microfiche from the Association of College Unions-International.

559 *Union Wire.* Published monthly by the Association of College Unions-International, Central Office, 400 E. Seventh Street, Bloomington, Ind. 47405.

This monthly newsletter features a general information exchange as well as late developing news and announcements. It is only available to ACU-I membership.

12

Career Development
and Placement Services

In the field of career services, the literature has dramatically increased during the past two decades. Prior to the early 1970s, career services offices on the nation's campuses had job placement as their primary, if not exclusive, function. The career services staff's duties consisted of gathering and maintaining placement files for graduating seniors and sometimes alumni, and the scheduling of interviews of the graduating job seekers by campus recruiters. These duties were primarily clerical in nature, although some public relations were involved in maintaining mutually beneficial relationships with recruiters. Occasionally, the staff gave some advice to job applicants regarding the development of a resume or job placement folder, or in deciding within which types of agencies or businesses the applicant might seek employment.

In the 1970s, however, employers began to have a decreased demand for college graduates, in part due to the increasing number of baby boomers flooding the job market. Students reacted by increasing the vocational emphasis in their undergraduate academic programs. They became more concerned earlier in their programs regarding their employability upon graduation. Furthermore, across the nation there was an increased emphasis upon student development in higher education. These factors combined to greatly change and increase the functions of the traditional placement bureau. The traditional function of assisting students to become employed was maintained but was expanded to provide help with a variety of job search strategies, such as cover letters, resumes, interviewing skills, networking programs, and the provision of a career/ employment library. To what originally had been occasional advice-giving services were added comprehensive support services for job-seeking students. Career services professionals took on the additional responsibility of marketing graduates, and this often included the recruitment and courtship of the college recruiters in an attempt to expand the number of potential job openings for graduates.

The career services offices have also become concerned that students are not thinking about employment until late in their senior year; consequently, they have geared their interventions to assist students in different phases of the career development process. Career libraries have been developed and stocked with information on various types of businesses, industries, and agencies. The libraries also house many other references covering career choice, specific occupational information, and career development materials. A variety of programs aimed at students in their earlier years on campus are designed to encourage career planning and decision making. In some cases, considerable career counseling activities have been implemented involving the use of a variety of psychological tests or computer-assisted career decision-making programs.

As the scope of services provided by the career services offices has increased, its boundaries have begun to overlap with other student services on campus. Some of the newer functions replicate services provided by campus counseling centers, and some institutions have faced decisions regarding where resources should be housed, which service should administer and interpret psychological tests, and which should have primary responsibility for career counseling. In many instances, however, the demand for career services has far outweighed the resources available in individual offices, and there has been little concern regarding the overlapping services.

The literature in the field of career services reflects these profound changes. The College Placement Council has produced numerous materials with much useful information dealing with these aspects of career services. In particular, model programs and services are reported in the *Journal of College Placement* (recently renamed the *Journal of Career Planning and Employment* (no. 613). In addition to the references cited in this chapter, there are a large number of popular books and pamphlets designed for the job seekers themselves. Most of these are how-to books, on such topics as how to find the right job for you, how to have a successful job interview, how to plan and undertake a successful career, and so on. The references cited in this chapter are those primarily useful to the professional on the college or university campus, and no attempt has been made to review the literally hundreds of books and pamphlets that have been produced to meet the concerns of the job seeker. Some of these are obviously of interest to the career services professional, and some are useful additions to the career services library. However, the quality of others is extremely questionable, and most career services professionals would agree that certain of these contain much poor and/or useless advice and information.

The variety of services now provided is also reflected in the literature cited, including the changes required by the Buckley Amendment in the operation of placement files and letters of reference. Part-time employment for college students has also been an aspect of some career services offices, while in other cases this function falls under the aegis of the student financial aid office. An additional function of placement offices, not shared by all, is the intermediary role between undergraduates and professional schools. Cooperative education programs have increased substantially in many institutions, and these also are often administered by the career services agency on the campus.

The overwhelmingly largest single source of periodical literature in the career services and placement field is the *Journal of Career Planning and Employment* (no. 613). Virtually all articles dealing with placement are found in that journal, while those dealing with career services and career development are often found in several counseling journals and in the *Journal of College Student Development* (no. 1). There may be a danger here in that placement professionals appear to communicate primarily among themselves through the *Journal of Career Planning and Employment* and through other placement publications. Many professionals in the placement field have received their training in areas other than in student development and perhaps feel little kinship with student affairs workers in other specialties. In any case they do not appear to communicate their ideas and research findings regarding college placement to other student affairs professionals in the generalist journals and are less likely to receive other ideas and findings from other student affairs professionals.

The references included in this chapter begin with those related to the organization and administration of career services offices. These are followed by a number of references related to career development, many of which are from the fields of counseling and vocational psychology. Sources of literature in the areas of career education, career information centers, and the technology in this field are followed by references dealing specifically with placement. A few references designed primarily for college recruiters (rather than career services professionals) have also been included. The periodical literature in the career services field is considerably more extensive than that in most other areas of student services, and brief descriptions of these periodicals that contain articles relevant to the student services field conclude the references in this chapter.

Organization and Programming

560 Beaumont, Andrea G.; Cooper, Alva C.; and Stockard, Raymond H. *A Model Career Counseling and Placement Program.* Bethlehem, Pa.: College Placement Services, 1980. 368 pages.

This third edition describes the various activities that are included in a career counseling and placement program, along with various issues and concerns. It includes examples of office forms and letters, job descriptions and guidelines for staffing, budgeting, ethics, and evaluation procedures.

561 Burck, Harman D., and Reardon, Robert (eds.). *Career Development Interventions.* Springfield, Ill.: Thomas, 1984. 356 pages.

This how-to book contains chapters concerned with establishing and delivering career development programs. It is designed for practitioners and discusses both the advantages and limitations of various approaches and strategies. Topics include use of texts, self-assessment, group approaches, use of computers, development of a career resource center, services for special populations, and ethical issues.

562 Scott, Gary J. *The Career Planning and Placement Office: Implications for the Future.* Bethlehem, Pa.: College Placement Council Foundation, 1983. 74 pages.

This publication reports the results of a survey of over 1,200 college and university placement directors regarding the college placement operations at their institutions. Topics covered include career development, vocational career development theory, evaluation of services, and model programs. Categories of service provided are categorized by size and public control in order that services on a particular campus can be compared with a national profile.

563 Scott, Gary J. *The Organization and Scope of College Relations and Recruiting.* Bethlehem, Pa.: College Placement Council Foundation, 1984. 255 pages.

This book summarizes a survey conducted among college recruitment managers and chief executive officers designed to assess the organization and scope of college relations and recruiting. This book contains numerous tables reporting the results of the study, along with brief narrative sections summarizing the results.

★564 Shingleton, John D., and Fitzpatrick, Edwin B. *Dynamics of Placement: How to Develop a Successful Career Planning and Placement Program.* Bethlehem, Pa.: College Placement Council Foundation, 1985. 200 pages.

This book contains information regarding planning and placement functions presented with ideas, programs, forms, and handouts designed to assist in the development of a comprehensive program.

565 Solmon, Lewis C. and Ochsner, Nancy, L. (eds.). *Using Longitudinal Data in Career Counseling.* New Directions for Education, Work, and Careers, no. 7. San Francisco: Jossey-Bass, 1979. 110 pages.

This sourcebook emphasizes the use of follow-up studies of students to help an institution improve career preparation programs. An explanation of how to create and use such institution-wide student data systems is included.

566 Watkins, Ed (ed.). *Preparing Liberal Arts Students for Careers.* New Directions for Education, Work, and Careers, no. 6. San Francisco: Jossey-Bass, 1979. 104 pages.

This volume demonstrates a way of offering a single effective and efficient career service for the liberal arts student. The major recommendation consists of coordinating career development programs that combine admissions, career counseling, and placement services.

Career Development

567 Astin, Alexander, W. *Four Critical Years: Effects of College on Beliefs, Attitudes, and Knowledge.* San Francisco: Jossey-Bass, 1977. 293 pages.

For a description of this work see entry no. 90.

568 Biller, Ernest F. *Understanding and Guiding the Career Development of Adolescents and Young Adults with Learning Disabilities*. Springfield, Ill.: Thomas, 1985. 180 pages.

For a description of this work see entry no. 402.

★569 Bolles, Richard N. *What Color Is Your Parachute?* Berkeley, Calif.: Ten Speed Press, 1989. 416 pages.

This book is the latest edition of the popular best-seller that outlines practical steps in choosing or changing careers. Its subtitle, "A Practical Manual for Job Hunters and Career Changers," describes the topics in the book that are presented in a very straightforward and easy-to-read form, which helps account for its popularity.

★570 Brown, Duane; Brooks, Linda; and Associates. *Career Choice and Development: Applying Contemporary Theories to Practice*. San Francisco: Jossey-Bass, 1984. 505 pages.

In the first portion of this book, authors of various theories of career choice have reviewed and updated their theories. In the second part, theories are examined in relation to specific groups such as those involved in midlife career changes, minorities, and women. Also included is a discussion of major issues in career development. Strategies are suggested for improving practices in a variety of settings and with different approaches. The use of tests and problem diagnosis is also explored, and recommendations for the achievement of an optimal match between the individual and job are presented.

571 Gordon, Virginia N. *The Undecided College Student: An Academic and Career Advising Challenge*. Springfield, Ill.: Thomas, 1984. 125 pages.

For a description of this work see entry no. 376.

572 Gutek, Barbara A. (ed.). *Enhancing Women's Career Development.* New Directions for Education, Work, and Careers, no. 8. San Francisco: Jossey-Bass, 1979. 107 pages.

This sourcebook explores factors affecting women's career development. A discussion of assessment tools and techniques for women's career planning and counseling is included.

★573 Gysbers, Norman C., and Associates. *Designing Careers: Counseling to Enhance Education, Work, and Leisure.* San Francisco: Jossey-Bass, 1984. 650 pages.

This publication of the National Vocational Guidance Association provides comprehensive information on career guidance, including the evolution of career development, the world of work today, knowledge bases of career development, practices and programs for facilitating career development, and emerging views of work and leisure.

★574 Hansen, L. Sunny, and Rapoza, Rita S. (eds.). *Career Development and Counseling of Women.* Springfield, Ill.: Thomas, 1978. 642 pages.

This edited volume contains twenty-six articles, most of which appeared previously in counseling and guidance journals dealing with women's career patterns. Included are articles dealing with the influence of sex role socialization and sex role stereotypes, female career decision making, and changing life-style and career patterns.

575 Harren, Vincent A.; Daniels, M. Harry; and Buck, Jacqueline N. (eds.). *Facilitating Students' Career Development.* New Directions for Student Services, no. 14. San Francisco: Jossey-Bass, 1981. 110 pages.

This sourcebook focuses on integrating career planning and preparation into students' education. It suggests the specific roles that faculty, student services, and others can play in career development.

★576 Herr, Edwin L., and Cramer, Stanley H. *Career Guidance Through the Life Span.* (3rd ed.) Boston: Little, Brown, 1987. 420 pages.

This book contains a general overview of career guidance. It discusses the various theories of career development and the various developmental stages of a person's career life.

577 Kapes, Jerome T., and Mastie, Marjorie M. (eds.). *A Counselor's Guide to Career Assessment Instruments.* (2nd ed.) Alexandria, Va.: American Association for Counseling and Development, 1988. 351 pages.

This volume represents a revision of the previous edition, entitled *Counselor's Guide to Vocational Guidance Instruments.* It includes a practical guide to forty-three of the most common career instruments and an annotated listing of an additional 126 others. Instruments include interest inventories, multiple aptitude batteries, personality measures, career maturity instruments, and combined assessment programs.

578 Katchadourian, Herant A., and Boli, John. *Careerism and Intellectualism Among College Students: Patterns of Academic and Career Choice in the Undergraduate Years.* San Francisco: Jossey-Bass, 1985. 324 pages.

For a description of this work see entry no. 95.

579 Leibowitz, Zandy B., and Lea, H. Daniel (eds.). *Adult Career Development: Concepts, Issues, and Practices.* Alexandria, Va.: American Association for Counseling and Development, 1986. 360 pages.

In this book pragmatic concepts, practical techniques, and relevant issues in helping adults negotiate changes in their careers are described. Training programs, strategies, and methods for a variety of settings are presented.

580	McKenzie, Ione L., and Manoogian-O'Dell, Margaret. *Expanding the Use of Students in Career Services: Current Programs and Resources.* Alexandria, Va.: American Association for Counseling and Development, 1988. 319 pages.

This monograph describes a program in which undergraduate students were selected and trained to offer educational and career services to their peers. Step-by-step guidelines for the selection and training of paraprofessionals are presented, along with descriptions of twenty-four model programs.

581	Miller, Juliet V., and Musgrove, Mary Lynn (eds.). *Issues in Adult Career Counseling.* New Directions for Continuing Education, no. 32. San Francisco: Jossey-Bass, 1986. 105 pages.

This volume details guidelines and strategies for facilitating career decision making for displaced or undirected adults. Special emphasis is placed on identifying self-esteem problems and designing appropriate interventions.

582	Montross, David H., and Shinkman, Christopher J. (eds.). *Career Development in the 1980s.* Springfield, Ill.: Thomas, 1981. 450 pages.

This edited volume includes work by thirty-four authors, most of them well known in the career development field. The first section of the book covers theories of career development. The second covers career development in higher education, and the third, career development in organizations.

583	Morgan, Marilyn A. *Managing Career Development.* New York: D. Van Nostrand, 1980. 384 pages.

This volume is a collection of readings organized with the assumption that careers develop over the course of one's career life and can be managed. The readings reflect how career issues differ for early, mid, and later career development and that career management is a shared process between the individual, the supervisor, and the organization.

★584 Osipow, Samuel H. *Theories of Career Development.* (3rd ed.) Englewood Cliffs, N.J.: Prentice-Hall, 1983. 339 pages.

This book summarizes and compares current theoretical approaches to vocational psychology. Existing theories are grouped into five categories: trait-factor theories, psychological theories, self-concept or developmental theories, personality-in-career theories, and behaviorally oriented social-learning approaches. Results of research of each type of theory and its implications for career counseling are included.

585 Shipton, Jane, and Steltenpohl, Elizabeth H. "Educational Advising and Career Planning: A Life Cycle Perspective." In Arthur W. Chickering and Associates, *The Modern American College: Responding to the New Realities of Diverse Students and a Changing Society.* San Francisco: Jossey-Bass, 1981, pp. 689–705.

The authors discuss elements of career development and career decision making. Emphasis is on the process by which adults make decisions regarding career changes, by taking into consideration previous experiences, current interests and values, employment opportunities and educational requirements. For a description of Chickering's complete work see entry no. 85.

586 van Aalst, Frank D. (ed.). *Combining Career Development with Experiential Learning.* New Directions for Experiential Learning, no. 5. San Francisco: Jossey-Bass, 1979. 104 pages.

This sourcebook focuses on combining career development and experiential education, and includes an explanation of career counseling tools used to meet the needs of individual students.

587 West, Jonathan T. *Career Planning, Development, and Management: An Annotated Bibliography.* New York: Garland Publishing, 1983. 325 pages.

This annotated bibliography contains brief summaries of publications that appeared between 1960 and 1982. Summaries are organized into three sections: career planning, career development, and career management.

★588 Yost, Elizabeth B., and Corbishley, M. Anne. *Career Counseling: A Psychological Approach.* San Francisco: Jossey-Bass, 1987. 265 pages.

This book presents a practical, step-by-step approach in which counselors can help their clients decide on careers best suited to their abilities and life-styles. The various factors that influence career choice and the various stages are presented, along with sample techniques, exercises, and work sheets.

Career Education

589 Harris, Norman, C., and Grede, John, F. *Career Education in Colleges: A Guide for Planning Two- and Four-Year Occupational Programs.* San Francisco: Jossey-Bass, 1977. 419 pages.

This guide deals with planning and operating college-level career education programs, including national goals and manpower needs, roles of colleges in career education, and the rate of return on individual investments in college.

★590 Hoyt, Kenneth B. *Career Education: Where It Is and Where It's Going.* Salt Lake City, Utah: Olympus Publishing, 1981. 401 pages.

This book presents a review of the history, philosophy, and current issues in career education. The use of the concept of career education in all educational settings, its importance in discussions of governmental acts and legislation, and the questionable value of a liberal arts education without entry-level occupational skills are examples of the topics and issues included by the author.

591 Rodgers, Ronald C. (ed.). *Measurement Trends in Career and Vocational Education.* New Directions for Testing and Measurement, no. 20. San Francisco: Jossey-Bass, 1983. 100 pages.

This sourcebook examines the new resources and techniques available for career guidance and assessment. Included is detailed information regarding ways to help young people select and enter the work force, matching skills of the job seeker to employment opportunities, and assessing on-the-job adjustment.

Career Information Centers

592 Aslanian, Carol B., and Schmelter, Harvey B. *Adult Access to Education and New Careers: A Handbook for Action.* New York: College Entrance Examination Board, 1980. 141 pages.

This book outlines the process of establishing an adult career information center. Included are examples of needed facilities, staffing, career materials collection, budgeting, and job descriptions.

Technology

593 Anderson, David L. *Computer Fundmentals: A Primer for Career Development Professionals.* Bethlehem, Pa.: College Placement Council Foundation, 1981. 51 pages.

This publication briefly describes how computers may be applied to career development. Included is an example of a computerized job notification/candidate information system and examples of other types of data that can be computerized in career services offices.

594 Cohen, Deborah P.; Cook, Sandy; Devlin, Thomas C.; and Maskin, Deborah R. *Video Technology in the Career Planning, Placement, and Recruitment Field.* Bethlehem, Pa.: College Placement Council, 1983. 102 pages.

This publication reports the results of a survey on audiovisual utilization in career planning and placement centers conducted by the staff of the Cornell University Career Center. Results summarize the extent to which audiovisual materials were being utilized in 1981 and includes a list of videotapes being used and a list of videotapes produced by employers. It also suggests how to supplement college recruitment efforts through the use of audiovisual materials.

595 Katz, Martin R. "SIGI: An Interactive Aid to Career Decision Making." *Journal of College Student Personnel,* 1980, *21,* 34–40.

This article briefly describes the System of Interactive Guidance and Information (SIGI), a computer program designed to assist students in making decisions regarding career choice. It describes the various exercises dealing with values, options, and decision-making strategies through which the student, seated at a computer terminal, is guided while working through an interactive program.

Placement

★596 Battle, Lynne D. *College Planning, Placement, and Recruitment Law: A Sourcebook for Practitioners.* Bethlehem, Pa.: College Placement Council, 1983. 190 pages.

This book presents information on laws that affect career planning, placement, and recruitment professionals. It covers the laws and regulations from the various acts and titles dealing with privacy, confidentiality, civil rights acts, age discrimination, equal pay acts, and information regarding typical state registration and licensing laws.

597 Blaska, Betty, and Schmidt, Marlin R. "Placement." In William T. Packwood (eds.), *College Student Personnel Services*. Springfield, Ill.: Thomas, 1977, pp. 368–421.

This review of the literature in the college placement fields is organized according to the following topics: philosophy, administration, programs, personnel, and relationships with other services. An extensive list of references is included. For a description of Packwood's complete work see entry no. 27.

598 Career Planning and Placement, University of Delaware. *Coloring Your Parachute: A Manual of Career Programs for Professionals*. Newark, Del.: University of Delaware Office of Career Planning and Placement, 1986. 164 pages.

This monograph provides information and materials related to the different types of programming conducted by career services offices. It contains outlines, information, and sample materials dealing with the marketing of programs, different types of workshops (such as resume preparations, job search strategies, interview preparation, and dress), and workshop evaluations. Handouts and transparencies for use in these programs are also included.

599 College Placement Council. *The Current Status of, and Reactions to, the Issues of Prescreening, Preselection, and Prerecruiting*. Bethlehem, Pa.: College Placement Council, 1985. 51 pages.

This monograph presents the results of a questionnaire survey of over a thousand college placement officials and a similar number of employers. The extent to which resume books are distributed, the extent to which each of the two groups practice prescreening and preselection for interview schedules, and the types of prescreening practiced are reported.

600 Gast, Linda K. *Career Decisions of Graduating Engineers.* Bethlehem, Pa.: College Placement Council Foundation, 1983. 47 pages.

This monograph presents the results of a study in which over a thousand bachelor's degree candidates in engineering at six different institutions completed three separate surveys concerned with why the students chose to pursue employment or graduate study, how they contacted particular employees or graduate schools, and why they accepted job offers from specific companies. The factors that are important to engineering students in making career plans and how these factors vary in the transition from education to employment are discussed.

601 LaMarre, Sandra E., and Hopkins, David M. *Career Values of the New Life-Style Professionals.* Bethlehem, Pa.: College Placement Council, 1984. 120 pages.

This monograph reports a study of the work attitudes, expectations of compensation, preferred job attributes, and job, family, and personal values of recent college graduates. Implications are suggested for career services professionals and for those who hire and supervise recent graduates.

602 National Society for Internships and Experimental Education. *The National Directory of Internships.* Raleigh, N.C.: National Society for Internships and Experimental Education, 1984. 315 pages.

This contains a directory of 400 internship programs with comprehensive information about each. The directory is organized by the type of organization offering the internship, but it is indexed geographically and functionally as well.

603 Task Force on Education and Employment. *Education for Employment: Knowledge for Action.* New York: Acropolis Books, 1979. 270 pages.

This report examines the job market changes and conditions that occurred during the 1970s and, based on that data, provides predictions and recommendations for the 1980s. It discussed the difficulty that nontechnical B.A.'s and liberal arts Ph.D.'s have experienced in the 1980s and the changing employment and training needs of future years.

College Recruitment

★604 Babbush, H. Edward; Bormann, Allen C.; Nance, Willis H.; and Thronson, Harley A. *College Relations in Recruiting: A Guide for Developing an Effective Program.* Bethlehem, Pa.: College Placement Council, 1982. 180 pages.

This volume is designed as a guide for those who recruit on the college campus, with sections dealing with selecting institutions, interviewing on campus, developing a college relations program, and following up with candidates.

605 Shingleton, John D., and Scheetz, L. Patrick. *Recruiting Trends, 1987–88.* East Lansing: Michigan State University Placement Services, 1987. 62 pages.

This monograph is a summary of the college recruiting trends survey conducted annually by the placement services office at Michigan State University. Over a thousand employers in business, government, and education were surveyed regarding the hiring trends for new college graduates, including salaries, campus recruiting activities, recruitment techniques, and other topics of interest to career services staff, personnel administrators, and job-seeking students. The monograph contains numerous tables and figures illustrating college recruitment practices and trends.

606 Thain, Richard J.; Yoxall, George J.; and Stewart, Richard A. *The Campus Connection: Effective College Relations and Recruiting.* New York: Brecker and Merryman, 1979. 91 pages.

This book outlines a college relations program for institutions that hire college graduates. It discusses the college recruitment program from initially developing campus contacts through selecting schools, interviewing candidates, and follow-up correspondence.

Periodicals and Annuals

607 *Business Week Careers.* A magazine published seven times a year by McGraw-Hill Inc. Business Week Careers, 5615 West Cermak Road, Cicero, Ill. 60650.

This magazine is primarily for college graduates seeking positions in business and industrial firms. In addition to providing information about careers in various fields and types of industries, it includes trends as to where the jobs are and covers other topics such as travel and dress.

608 *Career Development Quarterly* (formerly *Vocational Guidance Quarterly*). Published quarterly by the National Vocational Guidance Association, a division of the American Association for Counseling and Development, 5999 Stevenson Avenue, Alexandria, Va. 22304.

This quarterly contains articles dealing with research, theory, and practice in career development and career counseling.

609 *Careerism Newsletter.* A newsletter published monthly by WWWWW/Information Services Inc. WWWWW/Information Services Inc., Box 10046, Rochester, N.Y. 14610.

A multilith newsletter of twenty to twenty-five pages designed to provide current information regarding career and job opportunities, along with trends and prediction of future opportunities in a wide variety of career fields including business, industry, government, education, and health services. Entrepreneurial opportunities and trends in careers are presented in brief paragraphs emphasizing the most current data and predictions.

610 *CPC Annual.* Published annually by the College Placement Council, Inc., 62 Highland Avenue, Bethlehem, Pa. 18017. Approximately 950 pages.

This resource for college graduates, published annually over the past thirty years, provides employment information. It is published in three volumes, and a large number of copies are provided to each college member without charge. Volume One (approximately 100 pages) contains general information useful to job-hunting students. Volume Two (approximately 250 pages) lists career opportunities in business, administration, and other nontechnical fields. Volume Three (approximately 600 pages) covers opportunities in engineering, science, and computing.

611 *Directory of Career Planning and Placement Offices.* Published annually by the College Placement Council, 62 Highland Avenue, Bethlehem, Pa. 18017.

This directory lists the names of placement directors and assistant directors in institutions of higher education in the United States, along with information regarding the scheduling of recruitment interviews.

612 *Journal of Career Development.* Published four times a year by the Human Sciences Press, 72 Fifth Avenue, New York, N.Y. 10011.

This journal contains articles on career development theory, research, and practice. The focus is the impact of theory and research on practice.

★613 *Journal of Career Planning and Employment* (formerly the *Journal of College Placement*). Published by the College Placement Council Inc., 62 Highland Avenue, Bethlehem, Pa. 18017.

This quarterly journal is published by the College Placement Council. A subscription is included as a part of membership in the professional association. The journal includes a wide variety of articles, including those dealing with current issues, research studies in the field, career profiles, innovative programs or solutions to placement or recruitment problems, and profiles of notable personalities in the field. Subjects covered include recruitment and college relations, education and work force concerns, career information, and career counseling and placement. A number of publications and other media relevant for the field of career counseling and placement are reviewed in each issue.

★614 *Journal of Vocational Behavior.* Published bimonthly by the Academic Press Inc., One East First Street, Duluth, Minn. 55802.

This journal contains empirical and theoretical articles related to vocational development, choice, satisfaction, and effectiveness.

★615 *Spotlight.* A biweekly newsletter (twenty-one issues per year) published by the College Placement Council, 62 Highland Avenue, Bethlehem, Pa. 18017.

This newsletter is designed to inform career services professionals about news, legal issues, and trends in the field. A subscription is included with membership in the College Placement Council.

616 *Working Woman/McCall's.* Published monthly by Working Woman, P.O. Box 10130, Des Moines, Iowa 50340.

This magazine publishes career advice and articles of interest to employed women. Issues often include articles of interest to job-seeking college women and, occasionally, to college men as well.

∽ 13 ∾

Emerging Trends and Issues
in Practice and Research

In the introductions to the sources of literature in the previous chapters, certain characteristics and issues of the various student services functional areas have been enumerated and discussed. In this chapter seven different issues are considered that face the entire field and that will become increasingly important in the future.

Increasing Specialization and Consequent Separatism

As was mentioned in the introductory chapter, the trend within the student services field has been toward more and more specialization, with accompanying specialized professional competencies. As each of the specialty areas has developed its own literature in the form of newsletters, journals, handbooks, and with its own separate meetings and conventions, communication among the different student services fields is occurring with less and less frequency.

Journal subscriptions and memberships in professional organizations are costing increasing amounts of money so that each student services professional must choose from the various available organizations and their journals those which he or she will utilize most. With a limited amount of money and time to spend on professional activities, the tendency is to choose those organizations that provide information most useful on a day-to-day basis and to drop those organizations that are more general in nature. The exception to this is when an individual is seeking a new position either upon completion of graduate training or when planning a career shift into another student services area. Membership in generalist organizations and attendance at their national conventions becomes more likely when one is involved in a job search, but such memberships are dropped in favor of membership in the professional association that represents the specialty in which a new position has been obtained.

Reduced subscription rates to journals and newsletters for members of other student services associations is one method by which sources of literature can be used to communicate with those in other student service areas, but such policies have in the past met with only limited success.

One possible strategy in which the literature in the field could operate as a unifying factor would be the establishment of a journal for the entire student services profession. The American Association for Counseling and Development attempts to provide a journal that cuts across all the different counseling specialties and the American Psychological Association publishes the *American Psychologist,* which contains material designed to be of interest to all psychologists from laboratory experimental psychologists to private practicing clinical psychologists. Similarly, in student services a magazine or journal might be published that would contain articles from each of the student services specialties and that would also be of interest to those in the other specialties. Articles of interest to the entire field would also be included. To communicate adequately across the many specialties, the cost of subscribing to the periodical could be included in the membership dues of each of the different professional organizations.

Such a plan would require a great deal of cooperation among the national organizations — far more than has been characteristic in the history of these associations — but could be an effective antidote to the increasing fractionalization of the field.

Unequal Emphasis upon the Concept
of Student Development

During the next decade the literature in the student affairs field will contain considerable material dealing with the question of the application of developmental theories to day-by-day practices. Practitioners ask, "Now that I understand some of the student development theories, what do I do differently?" There is still much to be learned about this theory-to-practice question.

The concept of student development, as mentioned previously, has tended to provide at least a small unifying force in the face of many other forces that divide the field. But the student development concept has not been accepted with equal enthusiasm among all the different student services. Areas such as residence life, orientation, student activities, and counseling have readily accepted the concept and make use of it as professionals in their work with students. Other areas within student services such as admissions, financial aids, and international student advising make much less use of the concept, and these fields may become much more isolated from other student services.

It is possible that this concept may result in those services that are to be more developmental in their activities emerging more unified while those with less concern about student development may become more separate, both from each other and from the developmental services. The areas of student activities and residence life, in their shift away from custodial and control roles to new relationships with students, have readily incorporated the developmental philosophy into their activities. Staff involved in advising student activities went through a period during the activist years when they were heavily involved in dealing with student political/activist groups that consumed a major portion of their energies. Now, however, they are able to devote considerably more of their work to assisting students in their developmental growth.

Those working in the area of residence life have long been concerned with counseling and programming in the residence halls, and the developmental theories found a ready audience among these staff members. Those in either of the two areas of student activities or residence life who work with fraternities and sororities also saw the concept of student development as a broader, unifying concept that encompassed the types of leadership skills and interpersonal skills that they were attempting to teach throughout the Greek system. Similarly, those concerned with the orientation of new students saw orientation programs as an important link in the developmental process. For those professionals in career services, the career development aspect of their work involves important student development concepts, while their activities in regard to job finding and job placement are somewhat less developmental in nature.

Among other areas of student services, specialization and separation are more likely to occur. Financial aid professionals are developing an expanding literature base that deals heavily with grants, loans, and governmental policies. Many in the financial aid field believe they would like to take a more developmental approach to their work. They would prefer, for example, to be able to accomplish more financial counseling, but they typically feel that they are kept too busy with the many other aspects of their work. Any developmental work on their part must come after these aspects, and they find they seldom have the time to work on student development goals.

The field of admissions is becoming more sophisticated in the collection and use of information regarding the marketing of the institution and recruitment of students. As their knowledge base expands, admissions professionals will be able to take a more organized and effective approach to the recruitment and admissions processes. For admissions personnel in particular, however, the pressures will be on numbers rather than student development. With their own professional organizations and literature, they are much more likely to become separated from others in the student services field.

Work in the retention of students will also become increasingly knowledge based, better organized, and more professional. But those working in retention must deal with a variety of the other student services agencies on the campus and must also be concerned with the total development of the student.

Dealing with an Increasingly
Diverse Student Population

The range in ages of students is expanding on many college campuses as more and more older students return to the campus. These older students represent an extremely diverse population. While one of the older students is seeking to complete an undergraduate degree begun many years in the past, another is undertaking a graduate program that represents a significant midlife career change, a third may be a full-time homemaker planning to return to the job market, a fourth a professional enrolled in a course or workshop to keep up to date in his or her current field, and the fifth may be an elderly retiree enrolled in one or two courses purely for personal satisfaction. Policies appropriate for the full-time eighteen- to twenty-four-year-old student are obviously not likely to be appreciated by many of these diverse students, and one of the challenges facing student services professionals during the next several decades will be that of accommodating the extremely diverse student population that will be found on many campuses, especially those in or near urban areas.

It is also apparent that the student population will increasingly be made up of students from minority groups. In another decade minority groups will in fact become the majority on some campuses, and dealing with students from various minority cultures will be a significant challenge facing student services professionals.

On many campuses there is an attempt to create a sense of community among the students as well as a sense of community among those affiliated with a campus as a whole, including faculty, staff, and administrators. The presence of a diverse student population on the campus makes the building of a sense of community very difficult, and on some campuses almost impossible. Maintaining some sense of community with the diversity of students now appearing on the nation's campuses represents a challenge that those in student services will be attempting to meet one way or another during the next decade.

Moral and Ethical Values

There is currently concern by many that higher education is paying too little attention to the ethical and moral development of students as a part of the educational process. Questionable ethics on the part of certain educated professionals and duplicity among public servants have resulted in increased concern about the absence of moral education in the nation's schools and colleges. Higher education is criticized for graduating students who are too relativistic — students who have an easy tolerance for others' views and values without ethical and value commitments of their own. In answer to this criticism, certain of the professional schools have now added courses in ethics. Student services professionals concerned with the total development of students usually include the development of moral and ethical values among their concerns. While in the future some of the education in these aspects will take place in the classroom, there will likely also be an emphasis on a campus-wide approach that will undoubtedly involve student services professionals. After all, the efficacy of such training lies in a change in moral behavior outside the classroom. As a result of such training, are students less likely to be exploitive in their relationships with members of the opposite sex? Are they less likely to cheat on examinations? Are they more tolerant of others and less biased toward those from other cultures or ethnic groups?

Student services staff in certain fields can, if they choose to do so, provide a leadership role on the campus in attempting to promote ethical values. By modeling these values and by encouraging those activities that promote them, student services professionals can play an important role in helping to achieve ethical and just communities on the campus that can then have an impact and thus improve society at large.

Scholarship and Research

The Ph.D. is increasingly becoming a prerequisite for middle- and upper-level student services positions. As the number of professionals in the field with the competence to carry out significant research studies increases, the number of carefully conducted research studies should increase. So should the sophistication of student services professionals to understand and make use of the results of such research. The literature of the field in the future will therefore contain increasing numbers of reports of scholarly research studies in each of the specialty areas within the field.

The emphasis on student development within the student affairs profession is accompanied by a need for studies to focus on the personal and intellectual changes that students experience through these developmental processes. First, reasonably reliable and valid instruments with which to measure these developmental changes need to be devised. Then in order to adequately assess this development, relatively long-term interdisciplinary longitudinal studies of various developmental and behavioral characteristics of students are needed. The purpose of this research should be to (1) identify selected developmental needs of students enrolled at various institutions, (2) identify aspects of programs and services that promote student development, (3) identify aspects of programs and services that inhibit or counteract student development, and (4) suggest ways to improve programs and services to maximize student development.

Research is needed to distinguish elements of different campus environments and the impact these environments have upon students. In addition, the impact of various subenvironments on a campus also need to be studied, and one of the most important of these deals with student residences. Studies of the impact of different types of residence life and of different programs established within these residence units need considerable research if they are to be effectively undertaken and evaluated. Certain types of residence units such as fraternities, sororities, and co-ops have been on campuses for many years but have been the target of very little research, and they need to be studied.

In the field of admissions, studies concerned with the prediction of academic grades have been conducted for many years, with little improved prediction, and further studies to predict grades through correlation and regression techniques should have a very low priority. Research regarding student decision making as it affects the admissions process needs considerably more research, as do studies dealing with attrition and retention. Basic studies examining factors related to attrition have been repeated many times, but little is still known about the various combinations of factors—which vary greatly for each individual student—that lead to the decision to drop out of the institution.

Research on college students has shown that individuals' early perceptions of and reactions to institutions are extremely important and can color a student's entire collegiate experience. Most institutions recognize the importance of "getting off to a good start," and so most include various orientation programs and activities—some fairly simple, others extremely elaborate. The impact of these programs is largely unknown and even less is known about the differential impact of various types of orientation programs. Given the almost total lack of knowledge regarding the impact of these programs in spite of their universality and perceived importance, this topic represents a student services function that should receive considerable research activity.

Throughout the student services functional areas there is a need for outcome research. Such studies are difficult to conduct and usually are contaminated with many variables not easy to control. The measurement of change on any psychological variable among humans is always a difficult proposition. Nonetheless, as the emphasis upon accountability will continue into the future, many more outcome studies need to be conducted.

Standards of Professional Practice

A significant development within the student services profession has been the creation of the "CAS Standards" by the

Council for the Advancement of Standards for Student Services/Development Programs (see entry no. 183). This document provides some general standards and ethics for the general provision of services to students, along with standards and guidelines for sixteen of the functional areas within student services. For each of these functional areas, the standards for organization, necessary human resources, facilities, and evaluation are set forth. Standards for preparation programs for student service professionals at the master's degree level are also included. Although the Council for the Advancement of Standards has no certification or accreditation powers, these standards are expected to play an important role in the establishment of minimum standards in student services programs on the nation's campuses in future years. They will be used by student services professionals in evaluating their own programs and also as evidence to be presented to higher-level administrators on campuses as evidence for the need of additional resources to meet these standards. In addition, external review committees and accreditation bodies will undoubtedly use these standards as important references when they evaluate the student services programs on various campuses. For these reasons these standards are expected to contribute much to the student services profession as a whole and to raising the standards of the various functional areas on the nation's campuses.

Dealing with an Information Society

The universe of professional literature is continuing to expand, including the literature in the student services field. This expansion of professional literature is only a small part of the great expansion of information taking place in the society of the future into which we are being propelled. One of the major problems we all will face in an information society is attempting to deal with large amounts of information. The concept of information overload is already becoming a concern. The literature in the student services field will be affected in a number of ways by this information society and by its accompanying electronic media. Journals and newsletters may become less common as more materials are placed on compact disks and in computers, to be accessed electronically. What we now read in a printed journal we may obtain in the future first by doing a computer search into the area in which we are interested and then accessing electronically the particular article of interest, to be printed in our office. Journals that we now receive through the mail, in the future we may receive electronically. Already we are writing journal articles and research summaries on computer disks and sending them to journal editors and publishers. How long will it be before we receive our professional literature through that medium as well?

The expansion of information and the sources of that information is a trend that will affect most other professionals in important ways. Certainly the immense amount of information provided in an information society will tend to overload all those in higher education, including students. Student services professionals will have an additional responsibility to assist students in managing and sorting out the increasing amount of information that they will face on the campus. It is the student services professionals who will likely be required to take a leadership role on the college campus in dealing with this aspect of the coming information society.

This volume represents one means by which the literature in the student services field is made more manageable and more accessible to its professionals. It is expected that future literature in the field will contain both additional resources to assist professionals in their dealing with information overload within the profession and ideas, models, and studies that those in the student services field can utilize to assist students with this problem.

Name Index

Subject Index